Sino-Indian Relations
Contemporary Perspective

Sino-Indian Relations
Contemporary Perspective

Editors

R. Sidda Goud
Manisha Mookherjee

ALLIED PUBLISHERS PVT. LTD.

New Delhi • Mumbai • Kolkata • Lucknow • Chennai
Nagpur • Bangalore • Hyderabad • Ahmedabad

ALLIED PUBLISHERS PRIVATE LIMITED

Regd. Off.: 15 J.N. Heredia Marg, Ballard Estate, **Mumbai**–400001
Ph.: 022-22626476 • E-mail: mumbai.books@alliedpublishers.com

1/13-14 Asaf Ali Road, **New Delhi**–110002
Ph.: 011-23239001 • E-mail: delhi.books@alliedpublishers.com

17 Chittaranjan Avenue, **Kolkata**–700072
Ph.: 033-22129618 • E-mail: cal.books@alliedpublishers.com

751 Anna Salai, **Chennai**–600002
Ph.: 044-28523938 • E-mail: chennai.books@alliedpublishers.com

5th Main Road, Gandhinagar, **Bangalore**–560009
Ph.: 080-22262081 • E-mail: bngl.books@alliedpublishers.com

3-2-844/6 & 7 Kachiguda Station Road, **Hyderabad**–500027
Ph.: 040-24619079 • E-mail: hyd.books@alliedpublishers.com

60 Shiv Sunder Apartments (Ground Floor), Central Bazar Road,
Bajaj Nagar, **Nagpur**–440010

F-1 Sun House (First Floor), C.G. Road, Navrangpura,
Ellisbridge P.O., **Ahmedabad**–380006
Ph.: 079-26465916 • E-mail: ahmbd.books@alliedpublishers.com

Khasra No. 168, Plot No. 12-A, Opp. Wisdom Academy School,
Kamta, Surendra Nagar, **Lucknow**–227105
Ph.: 09335202549 • E-mail: lko.books@alliedpublishers.com

Website: www.alliedpublishers.com

ISBN: 978-93-85926-22-8

Published by Sunil Sachdev and printed by Ravi Sachdev at Allied Publishers
Pvt. Ltd., (Printing Division), A-104 Mayapuri Phase II, New Delhi-110064

Foreword

China is India's obsession. Whether the obverse is true is doubtful. Almost all the Indian foreign policy contours are preeminently dominated by one singular poser: How to tackle China, its power, economic competitiveness, security threat, strategic capability and reach. The challenge of coping with Asia's largest and world's second largest economic power is compounded by the fact of China's ambitious and frequent multilateral plans. Each of the Chinese plans, regional and global, bears the political and economic ambitions of the East Asian giant, shrouded though in persuasive language and luring dividends. BCIM, MSR, Asian Silk Road, Asian Infrastructure Investment Bank, BRICS Bank are sound international narratives conjuring a peaceful and friendly world of shared political and economic bonds and interests. Each proposal aims at integrating the global markets through networks of connectivities eventually integrating the Asian economies with global economy. Ingenious and attractive, these plans are floated by China in a complimentary sense, not competitive. Both friends and adversaries or perceived adversaries of Beijing are invited to join them.

Precisely such plans as the above in their content and reach, pose dilemmas to India. Should India support or stay out of the Chinese regional and globally overarching plans. If India rejects, the world tries to attribute negativism to the Indian foreign policy psyche or at least China will send such messages. Should India chose to join the plans, there is always a lurking skepticism that the Chinese models of cooperation are aimed at curbing the Indian political and strategic objectives in the Indian Ocean, Asia-Pacific (India-Pacific; Asia-India-Pacific are the recent substitutes) and the world at large. Chinese plans also compel India's quick policy response.

Non-response or delayed acceptance of a Chinese regional plan like the BCIM or MSR can bypass India while others, immediate neighbours and distant friends of India would be drawn into the seemingly attractive Chinese projects. Surely such a scenario does not augur well to a growing power like India which has wider strategic and economic interests in the Indian Ocean Region (IOR) and beyond. Hence, China-led initiatives of regional/global cooperation compel quick Indian policy responses.

India therefore is under constant compulsion to search for policy options to answer the Chinese ambitious plans. The options could be to formulate policies which can effectively counter the Chinese; apply diplomatic tactics to discourage or wean away other powers, small and big, from subscribing; join the Chinese projects but redefine their terms to suit Indian interests; or, simply adopt an insular posture. The last option as already indicated will be disastrous as it would isolate India while China, the ambitious and powerful might succeed in mobilizing larger number of supporters backing its project networks creating thereby strong constituencies to the Chinese power and presence in Indian Ocean. The trend is rather already evident going by the positive responses to the Chinese plans by countries like Bangladesh, Maldives and Sri Lanka. Ambitious country like India with great power notions should not remain insular from the compulsive dynamics of power transition led by China.

I hope some of these issues raised above pertinent and inescapable, have received fair attention by the papers in this compiled volume. In a sheer sentimental sense, I am pleased that the Centre for Indian Ocean Studies is keeping the tradition of research publication, a noble trend initiated by my predecessors and me as the CIOS Directors.

P.V. Rao
Emeritus Professor of Political Science
Osmania University

Contributors

1. **Dr. G.V.C. Naidu**, Professor in the Centre for Indo-Pacific Studies, School of International Studies, JNU, New Delhi. He specializes in Asia-Pacific issues, Southeast Asian affairs, Japanese foreign and security policies, maritime security, and the Indian Ocean. Visiting Professor at the Daito Bunka University, Japan, Gakushuin University Tokyo; National Chengchi University, Taipei, a visiting fellow at the East-West Center, Honolulu; at the Japan Institute of International Affairs, and a Research Fellow at the Institute of South-East Asian Studies, Singapore.

2. **Seshadri Vasan** is Commodore, Indian Navy (Retd.) Head, Strategy and Security Studies, Centre for Asia Studies, India, Director, Asian Secretariat World Boderpol (WBO), An alumnus of the Defence Services Staff College and the College of Naval Warfare, India. A Director at the Naval Aviation Staff, Aviation Planning, Operations and Training. He was as a faculty at the prestigious Naval War College that trains senior level officers from all the three services. He is a member of the Maritime Security Programme at the Observer Research Foundation, a major think tank in India. Director of the Asian Secretariat of the World Borderpol (WBO). Presently the Director, Chennai Centre for China Studies.

3. **Prof. Yagama Reddy**, Emeritus Professor, Centre for South East Asian and Pacific Studies, Sri Venkateshwara University, Tirupati. Authored 8 books and edited 5 books. Prof. Reddy served as the Chairman, the Board of Studies (2001–05) as well as the Director (2005–2006

and 2008-2010) of the Centre for Southeast Asian & Pacific Studies, and the Vice-Principal, College of International Studies of S.V. University. He also served as Public Relations Officer and Dean, University Development of S.V. University. Prof. Reddy was the awardee of the Australia-India Council (AIC) Fellowship (2005) that facilitated his visit to a consortium of Australian Universities and Institutes. He was also conferred Honorary Research Associate of Monash University, Melbourne (Australia). He was also a member of the UGC Advisory Committee on Area Studies Programme, New Delhi, and a member of Board of Studies in South and Southeast Asian Studies and Defense and Strategic Studies— Nautical Science, University of Madras as well as member of Advisory Committee of the UGC Centre for Indian Ocean Studies, Osmania University, Hyderabad.

4. **Dr. Sidda Goud**, Professor of Economics at UGC Centre for Indian Ocean Studies and Director of the Centre, Osmania University, Hyderabad. During 2003-2005, he was served as a Member, Executive Council of Osmania University. He was awarded Ph.D. from Department of Economics, Osmania University in 1989 and he has been guiding Ph.D. and M.Phil scholars in the Department of Economics, Osmania University. He has authored the book 'Agriculture, Trade Economic Development' (2005): and three occasional papers (i) 'India Needs a Comprehensive Inflation Index', (February 2011), (ii) 'Impact of Global Warming on Indian Ocean Countries', (July 2011), (iii) 'Micro Finance (MFs) Impact in India: A Study in Andhra Pradesh' (July 2013). He is the Editor of the book "India-Sri Lanka Relations: Strengthening SAARC" published by Allied Publishers, New Delhi (2013), He is the Editor of the book "India and Iran in Contemporary Relations" published by Allied Publishers, New Delhi (2014), and also is the Editor of the Bi-annual

Journal *Indian Ocean Digest*, published by the UGC Centre for Indian Ocean Studies, Osmania University, Hyderabad.

*Manisha Mookherjee, Associate Professor of Sociology, UGC Centre for Indian Ocean Studies, Osmania University, Hyderabad. She has attended and participated in various National and International Conferences/ Seminars and has published research papers in various Indian Journals of Sociology, Urban Studies and Population Studies and in edited books. She has authored two country monographs. Her areas of Interest are: Urban Sociology and Urban Studies, Demography Environmental Issues—Pollution and Public Health, Development and Displacement Issues, and issues related to South Asia. Co-editor of the book "India and Iran in Contemporary Relations" published by Allied Publishers, New, "China in Indian Ocean Region' published by Allied Publishers, New Delhi and Associate Editor of the Bi-annual Journal *Indian Ocean Digest* published by the UGC Centre for Indian Ocean Studies, Osmania University, Hyderabad.

5. **Dr. M. Mayilvaganan**, Assistant Professor, International Strategic & Security Studies, National Institute of Advanced Studies (NIAS), Indian Institute of Science (IISc) Campus, Bangalore.

6. **Sylvia Mishra**, A Researcher with the ICRIER-Wadhwani Chair in India-US Policy Studies, ICRIER, New Delhi. Was a member of an Expedition to Central Asia to promote Track II Diplomacy supported by Ministry of External Affairs and India Central Asia Foundation. Research interests include Foreign Policy, Security and Defense Studies and South Asian and Middle Eastern Politics. Co-authored the ICRIER-Wadhwani Report

'India-US Defence Industrial Cooperation: The Way Forward' Edited 'Studies on Iran' and 'Studies on Pakistan', published by Foreign Policy Research Centre, New Delhi.

7. Amrita Jash, is a Doctoral Candidate in Chinese Studies, at the Centre for East Asian Studies, School of International Studies, Jawaharlal Nehru University, New Delhi-India.

8. Dr. Radha Raghuramapatruni, Associate Professor in Economics & International Business, GITAM School of International Business, GITAM University, Visakhapatnam-45. Associate Professor—International Trade and Economics... Double Gold Medalist in Economics from Andhra University, Visakhapatnam, her Specializations are International Trade and Trade Theories; Business Environment and Policy; Global Economic Environment; Micro and Macro Economics; Environmental Economics.

9. Dr. Durga Bhavani is an researcher in the area of International Relations. A member of the Board of Studies in Andhra Mahila Sabha Arts and Science College for Women, Hyderabad. She has vast experience in teaching in the areas of political science and international relations.

10. Dr. Sukalpa Chakrabarti, Associate Professor (IR & Public Policy) Deputy Director, Symbiosis School of Economics, Symbiosis International University, Pune. Her research interests include conflicts in West Asia, India's West Asia policy, politics and foreign policy of Iran, Iraq and Israel, and issues relating to democratization in the region. She has published West Asia: Civil Society, Democracy and State (New Delhi, 2010), several research papers, book and articles.

Preface

The Modi government has accorded greater priority to improve relations with China not withstanding the fact that the long pending border disputes are yet to be settled. Prime Minister Modi's objective is that Sino-Indian collaboration will help in contributing to India's economic ambition of achieving rapid growth rate. Such expectations seem to override the other bilateral irritants with China which include frequent border clashes and the strategy of containing India strategically in Indian Ocean. Accordingly, India joined China's sponsored multilateral institutions like the Asian Infrastructure Investment Bank (AIIB) as a founding member and has shown interest in Bangladesh-China-India-Myanmar (BCIM) economic corridor.

However, India has reservations on China's Maritime Silk Road and China Pakistan Economic Corridor (CPEC), the latter passing through Indian territory in Pakistan Occupied Kashmir (POK). The Modi government desires to go with India's maritime scheme called 'Mousam' instead of joining China's Belt and Road project. Some scholars hold the view that India should join China's MSR project to gain the economic benefits from it.

Chinese President Xi Jinping revived and accelerated the Road and Belt projects primarily to boost the country's manufacturing sector and improve its trade relations with Southeast Asian neighbours. Xi mooted these mega projects during his visit to Kazakhstan in 2013. Since then several countries in the Eurasian Belt evinced keen interest in them. However, India has so far not made up its mind and cited lack of clarity as the reason for hesitation. China has been financing many projects under the Silk Road scheme to interested countries like Pakistan, Sri Lanka and others.

China is also subtly involving in easing India-Pakistan tensions within the multilateral framework of the Shanghai Cooperation Organization (SCO). Chinese scholars recognize that Beijing has to impart greater balance in its ties with India and Pakistan. Chinese are also conscious of the need of India's support for these projects in the Indian Ocean region. MSR is an integral part of China's ambition to forge economic integration of Eurasia under its auspices. This is a part of China's long term goal of emerging as a global rival to the US. Following are the major infrastructure projects envisaged under the rubric of MSR:

1. 3000 km China-Pakistan Economic Corridor from Kashgar to Gwadhar port in Pakistan which is passing through the POK, is a 46 bn USD project funded by China.
2. 2800 km Rail/Road Project from Kunming (China) to Kolkata (India) via Myanmar, Bangladesh called BCIM corridor.
3. 1215 km Rail/Road corridor project from Yunnan (China) to the port of Kyankpya (Myanmar).
4. 741 km Rail corridor from Lhasa (Tibet) to Kathmandu (Nepal) and to Patna (Bihar-India).
5. 5000 km Naning (China) to Singapore Economic Corridor.

The Naning-Singapore Economic Corridor, an initiative of China is also called as China-Indo-China Peninsula International Corridor, started in 210 with a core initiative aimed at economic integration to eight cities in South China with Naning in China, Hanoi and Ho Chi Minh in Vietnam, Vientiane in Laos, Phnom Penh in Cambodia, Bangkok in Thailand, Kuala Lumpur in Malaysia and Singapore, with modern road, rail, pipelines as well as have cross-borders connectivity. The corridor is planned to better connect China with ASEAN economies and encourage development across the whole region as an enroute to the emergence of an ASEAN-China Free Trade Area in the near future. The corridor being is structured to help China, which aims to revamp its economy to a more developed "new normal" plain, and to shift its excess manufacturing capacity to the less developed zones in the ASEAN.

The Symposium had the following themes:

- *Road and Belt Mega Project:* Interplay of Economics and Politics
- *Asian Infrastructure Investment Bank (AIIB):* Role and Reach
- New Development Bank of BRICS: Problems and Prospects
- *China—A Link between Eurasia and Indian Ocean:* Analysis of China's Geo-Strategy
- *India-China Equation:* India's Dilemma—Containment cum Cooperation; China's Choices; Views of ASEAN Countries, Japan, USA, Russia, etc.

Editors

R. Sidda Goud
Manisha Mookherjee

Acknowledgements

This book is an outcome of the National Symposium on 'India-China Relations: Recent Developments', held on 28th–29th December 2015, organized by UGC Centre for Indian Ocean Studies, Osmania University, Hyderabad.

While we would like to thank a number of people who have encouraged and supported us in bringing out this volume, a few deserve special mention. First and foremost our deepest gratitude to Smt. Ranjeev R. Acharya, (I/c), Vice-Chancellor Osmania University, Hyderabad, Prof. E. Suresh, Registrar, Osmania University, Hyderabad for promptly accepting and granting permission to conduct the National Symposium on 'India-China Relations: Recent Developments'. A special mention of gratitude to the Advisory Committee Members of the UGC Centre for Indian Ocean Studies for their support and encouragement to conduct the Symposium and for their keen interest and participation.

We express our sincere thanks and gratitude to a host of dignitaries who graced the occasion. We are grateful to Prof. T. Tirupathi Rao, former Vice-Chancellor, Osmania University, Hyderabad and Prof. A. Ravindra Nath, Dean, Development & UGC Affairs, Osmania University, Hyderabad for accepting as Guest of Honour for the Inaugural Session. We also express our gratitude and thanks to Prof. P.V. Rao, former Director, UGC Centre for Indian Ocean Studies for his constant support, guidance and participation in the Symposium. We feel honoured and privileged to have one of our long standing well-wisher Prof. Yagama Reddy, Emeritus Professor, Centre for Southeast Asian & Pacific Studies, Sri Venkateshwara University,

Tirupati for accepting our invitation, Commodore (Retd.) Seshadri Vasan, presently Director, Strategy and Security Studies, Centre for China Studies, Chennai, and to all the distinguished delegates.

We deeply appreciate the contributors for their sincere academic support by participating in the National Symposium and subsequently submitting the revised papers for publication. The freedom of expression of the contributors have been taken care of and not subdued in the process of editing their papers; thereby the views expressed in these papers are essentially of those of the authors and not of the editors.

We would also like to place on record our acknowledgements to UGC, Osmania University, Indian Council of Social Science Research (ICSSR), Osmania University, Hyderabad and State Bank of Hyderabad, Arts College Branch, Osmania University, Hyderabad. We also express our thanks to Osmania University authorities, faculty members and the non-teaching staff of UGC Centre for Indian Ocean Studies, Osmania University, Hyderabad.

R. Sidda Goud
Manisha Mookherjee

Contents

BCIM Economic Corridor and Prospects for India-China Cooperation

G.V.C. Naidu

INTRODUCTION

Contrary to the past when much of the discourse on India-China relations was overwhelmingly confined to three aspects, that is, the complex border/territorial dispute, China's close links with Pakistan, especially in the military and nuclear fields, and the Dalai Lama issue, now there is a remarkable shift the relationship is witnessing. Although the above-mentioned problems still remain, numerous other develop-ments in the past decade and a half are overshadowing them and thus the relationship is witnessing an unprecedented transformation. This is because several other issues are beginning to dominate the bilateral agenda, such as bilateral economic relations, global trade talks, regional security in the Asia-Pacific and Indian Ocean regions, a variety of common non-traditional security challenges, in particular, terrorism and piracy, and global multilateral trade negotiations. Both of them have created several institutional mechanisms, Strategic Economic Dialogue, India-China Defence and Security Dialogue, Maritime Affairs Dialogue, etc., for instance, to engage each other more robustly.

One dimension that seems to be playing a key role in influencing the India-China bilateral relations relates to the unfolding East Asian economic and security architecture and the problems associated with. No question that economic issues and the geostrategic imperatives that are resulting in as a consequence are dominating the discourse despite disputes in the South China Sea and East China Sea hogging limelight. The recently concluded Trans-Pacific Partnership (TPP), if ratified by the respective governments (in particular by the US Congress), will certainly be a game changer in terms of how regional economic relations would shape up in the coming year. And the other significant developments are the talks to finalise a pan-East Asian Regional Comprehensive Economic Partnership (RCEP) and innumerable bilateral and multilateral free trade agreements that have been entered into. All these will aid in not only in enhancing intra-regional economic cooperation but will also advance regional economic integration, a process that is already underway in a big way.

Against the above backdrop, India is still a marginal player from the perspective of East Asia in terms of its economic significance to the region although from an Indian perspective nearly 27 percent of its trade is conducted with this region. Hence, it needs to qualitatively enhance its role and involvement in East Asian economic vibrancy by making use of every opportunity that arises. In the economic dynamism that is sweeping East Asia, subregional multilateral frameworks such as Association of Southeast Asian Nations (ASEAN), Bangladesh-China-India-Myanmar (BCIM), China-Japan-S. Korea Dialogue, Greater Mekong Subregion (GMS), etc., are becoming key drivers of regional economic cooperation and integration.

Even though it was created more than a decade and a half back, only now that the BCIM is coming to the centre stage as member countries realize that it can play a unique role in increasing economic cooperation among themselves and with the rest of the region. It is clear that a successful BCIM economic cooperation venture would enable India to be a significant part of East Asian economic architecture. An added advantage is that China's ambitious Belt and Road Initiative, which would entail huge investments in connecting vast regions across the continents, will help in creating appropriate infrastructure without which it will not succeed. Hence, there is an urgent need to recast India-China relations discourse with a greater focus on economic engagement, for it will be the principal determinant of the Indo-Pacific's new order. In the following, the paper would briefly discuss certain aspects such as the rise of East Asia and its rapidly growing economic integration, the role of BCIM in this context, and why BCIM matters to India in terms of its role in enhancing India's economic links with East Asia in general and China in particular and in reorganizing India-China relations since these two countries are likely to be major players in the region from a longer-term point of view.

EAST ASIA'S RISE

Something remarkable is happening in terms of economic relations across the globe in general but more prominently in Asia. No question that global centre of gravity is invariably shifting to Asia. If China's unprecedented rise to a large extent and India to a lesser extent constitutes cynosure of much of the discourse, not many pay attention to the fact that the entire East Asian region is on the rise. According to economic historians, China and India together constituted more than 50% of global GDP before the onset of colonialism. The traditional trading patterns and economic linkages among the countries of East Asia, especially between India and China, besides massive cultural, religious and linguistic interactions, that thrived for over two thousand years were badly disrupted due to colonial interests. Never once there was an occasion of clash of interests between these two Asian giants and they existed peacefully without ever stepping on each other's toes. So far, much of what is said mostly relates to the rise and fall of great powers but it is unprecedented that such a vast region such as East Asia comprising some 50 percent of the global population on the rise. 3 out of 4 largest economies are located in this region. China is the largest trading and manufacturing nation and possesses largest foreign exchange reserves. Japan is super power in advanced technologies and has private savings of about US $ 14 tr., 4 tr. pension, and another 4 tr. foreign assets. India's story is yet to fully unfold-leader in niche areas IT, huge human resource base, massive demographic advantage. Not just China, Japan and India, even smaller powers are extremely vibrant and are playing significant role economically. South Korea, Singapore, Hong Kong and Taiwan with a combined populations of just 85 mn. have 1.5 tr. foreign exchange reserves. East Asia is emerging as the global engine of growth and hence, what happens here will have implications for the rest of the world. The region already holds more than half the world's foreign exchange reserves and accounts for nearly a quarter of financial assets. It has logged double the average world's growth rates and indications suggest that buoyant outlook will continue for foreseeable future.

Along with the rise of East Asia, there are also other interesting developments taking place, the most prominent being greater economic cooperation and economic integration within the region. Currently, a large number of FTAs are under implementation and several more are under negotiation, besides the TPP and RCEP. There is a sea change in trading patterns: the intra-East Asian trade has increased from 35% in 1980 to around 56% by 2014, and is growing. It is already more than intra-regional trade in North America and the way it is growing it may surpass even the European Union. Similarly, the intra-regional levels of FDI are also increasing rapidly: from around 16 in 1991 to more than 80 percent by the late 2000s. It means two things: one, the East Asian market is expanding much faster and simultaneously the overall importance of markets outside the region, in particular, North America and the EU, is steadily declining, and two simply because economic opportunities are huge in East Asia, investments too increasingly are getting concentrated within the region. Thanks to the deadlocked WTO Doha Round talks, the trend towards regional arrangements to take advantage of buoyant economic environment in the East Asian region is rapidly growing leading to, as noted hundreds of Regional Trading Agreements (RTAs). Of course, strong economic bonds in the region also have a major on political considerations-diplomatic dividends strong economic links accrue too are driving the process. As of September 2012 in East Asia, there were 103 FTAs in effect involving one or more countries from the region, most of them bilateral. There are another 26 signed FTAs, 64 under negotiation and 60 more proposed. Most of these, in fact, are far more expansive with ambitious objectives than simply to promote trade. These are mostly Comprehensive Economic Partnership/ Cooperation Agreements. As a result, there is even a talk of building an East Asian 'community', which would have been far-fetched even a decade back. Market dynamics, which had been the primary driver of burgeoning intra-regional economic linkages, is now being complemented by the newly created regional institutions. Hence, attempts to create pan-East Asia trading blocks. Thus, RCEP along with ASEAN Economic Community will have great impact.

According to the Asian Development Bank, the "Regional Cooperation and Integration (RCI) is a process by which national economies become more interconnected regionally. RCI plays a critical role in accelerating economic growth, reducing poverty and economic disparity, raising productivity and employment, and strengthening institutions. It narrows development gaps between Asia's developing member countries by building closer trade integration, intraregional supply chains, and stronger financial links, enabling slow-moving economies to speed their own expansion."

INDIA-EAST ASIA ECONOMIC RELATIONS

The next issue what is the status of India's economic relations with East Asia. In 2013–14, India's trade with South Asian Association for Regional Cooperation (SAARC) member states was just 7%; with EU 13% and with the ASEAN+5 (ASEAN ten countries, China, Japan, South Korea, Australia, New Zealand) comprised 28%. Among all the major trading partners, India's trade has been growing the fastest with East Asian countries (ASEAN+5) than any other region. Furthermore, some of the major investors are from East Asia. Hence, there is no question that India's economic future lies in East Asia. However, economics also happens to be the weakest link in India's Look East policy. That economically it is still a marginal power compared to other great powers is apparent when one compares India and China trade with ASEAN: in 2013–14 India-ASEAN was just $ 74 bn compared to China's 401 bn. Undoubtedly, India is underperforming in realizing its trade potential. A major impediment is poor connectivity and low-level of integration with rest of East Asia. It needs to be understood that strong economic stakes are defining the traditional notion of security. Although the region is well known for its enormous diversity and lacking a single common characteristic, besides vast disparities in economic development, shared interest in enhancing economic prosperity is having great impact on the way countries interact with each other. True, there are several tricky and sensitive territorial disputes, vestiges of historical animosities still linger and quite often nationalist tendencies come to the fore, yet the region has, by and large, remained stable and peaceful barring some very minor incidents. The only logical reason that can be attributed to this is huge economic interests. Economic development cannot be expected to take place successfully unless the region remains peaceful. Despite all the heat that either the Senkaku or South China Sea disputes generate, it is most unlikely that a major armed conflict would break out, for the consequences both regional stability and economic development would be catastrophic. Seen in this backdrop, the salience of BCIM becomes clear.

INDIA AND BCIM FORUM FOR REGIONAL ECONOMIC COOPERATION

It needs to be recognized that fundamental shifts in India's thinking are taking place. Now there is the greater realization that New Delhi is lagging behind economically compared to other East Asian countries. In East Asia, whereas the Southeast Asian countries are creating an ambitious ASEAN Economic Community, China-Japan-South Korea Economic Co-operation has been under discussion. In response to RCEP and not to be left out of the regional integration attempts, the U.S. is seriously pursuing the so-called 'high standard', '21st century' Trans-Pacific Partnership (TPP) proposal, which, if successfully negotiated, would create a mega market. Yet another proposal to create a pan-Asia Pacific trading bloc called Free Trade Agreement in Asia Pacific (FTAAP) was approved in principle during the 2014 Asia-Pacific Economic Cooperation (APEC) summit meeting held in Beijing. RCEP is the only region-wide proposal that India is involved so far. India has to increase its leverages in an increasingly inter-dependent region.

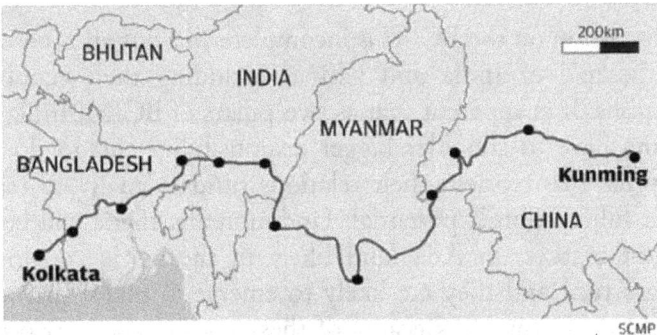

Fig. 1: Proposed BCIM-Economic Corridor

The issue is why the BCIM matters to India now than ever before. Probably one of the backward and least integrated with the rest of India is the Northeast. It along with West Bengal is virtually left out of the Look East policy. The border trade with Myanmar is minuscule-0.006% of India's East Asian trade. Further, the Northeast has neither market nor industry, and local products have not been leveraged properly. Given its geographical location, the Northeast needs to look for markets beyond India. However, poor connectivity has been a bane for Northeast. To reap the economic benefits, transport corridors need to be built. Fortunately, the Modi government is showing enormous interest in the development of the Northeast. He talked in terms of building economic corridors. Therefore, in addition to the other corridors that New Delhi is building, the BCIM economic corridor too becomes key in order not only help develop the Northeast, which is the best way to remove the feeling of alienation that the people of this region have been harboring for a long time but also to decrease the lure of insurgency and bring about political stability. Of course, while this BCIM corridor provides access to the large Indian market for Chinese goods, Beijing needs to address concerns about the ballooning trade deficit and fears of dumping of products.

INDIA, CHINA AND BCIM

A discussion on the BCIM is incomplete without an assessment of the role of India and China, including their economic relations. It is apparent that as two pillars of BCIM, India and China have to shoulder bigger responsibility and to do that they have to reorient their relations fundamentally to realize their full economic potential. Undoubtedly, theirs will be the largest markets in Asia (and likely in the world too in the longer run) and they are likely to emerge as major drivers of global development. Because of these reasons, these two have initiated an India-China Strategic Economic Dialogue.

Moreover, they are in the forefront in reordering global financial relations dominated by Bretton Woods system since 1944. The Asian Infrastructure Investment Bank (AIIB) and the BRICS Bank can be considered as first steps toward a New Global Economic Order.

China is beginning to emerge as a major investor in India. The agreement signed during President Xi Jinping visit to India in September 2014 that committed China to invest $ 20 bn. followed by another agreement entered into when Prime Minister Narendra Modi visited China in May 2015 for another 24 bn. investments in India will make much difference both to their perceptions about each other as well as strengthening economic links, which will scale up stakes in each other.

Specifically with respect to the BCIM, the Joint Statement issued during Premier Li Keqiang's 2013 visit stated the creation of a Joint Study Group on strengthening connectivity in the BCIM region for closer economic, trade, and people-to-people linkages and to initiating the development of a BCIM Economic Corridor. The "proposed corridor could run from Kunming (China) in the east to Kolkata (India) in the West, broadly spanning the region, including Mandalay (Myanmar), Dhaka and Chittagong (Bangladesh) and other major cities and ports as key nodes... With the linkages of transport, energy and telecommunication networks, the Corridor will form a thriving economic belt that will promote common development of areas along the Corridor" (minutes of 1st Joint Study Group, December 2013).[1]

BCIM AND CHINA'S BELT AND ROAD

Beijing has announced an ambitious, grand project to build the Silk Road Economic Belt and Maritime Silk Road. Vice Premier Zhang Gaoli announced that China would invest $ 900 bn on Belt and Road, and the "corridors are set to run through China-Mongolia-Russia, New Eurasian Land Bridge, China-Central and West Asia, Indo-China Peninsula, China-Brazil, and Bangladesh-China-India-Myanmar." Zhang underlined that "connectivity" concerns not only physical infrastructure like roads but also people-to-people exchanges, policy coordination, trade and capital flows, etc. There is a lack of clarity on China's Maritime Silk Road plans since details have not been spelled out. In any case, the meeting point for the Silk Road Economic Belt and Maritime Silk Road is Kolkata. Here BCIM connectivity is the crucial link connecting the Belt and Road. Simultaneously, an urgent need to build political trust and dispel misperceptions is needed to fructify the Belt and Road projects. India and China should follow the strategy of cherry-picking than harping on differences. Once these mega projects bear fruit and Asia economically integrates itself more vigorously, it will radically change the way the world conducts its economic relations and Asia will recapture its pre-eminent status once again.

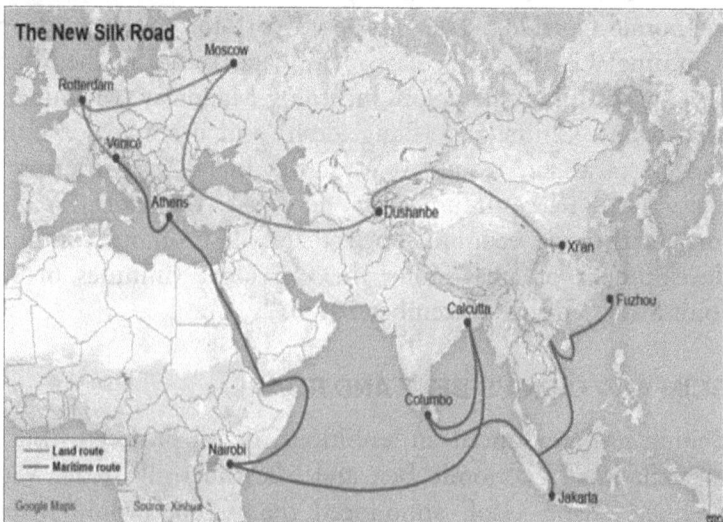

Fig. 2

As far as the BCIM is concerned, it has to evolve its own model than emulate sub-regional frameworks such as Greater Mekong Sub-region or BIMSTEC since each is unique because of unique circumstances and objectives. What is required is that the BCIM has to make its objectives clear. A concrete plan of action for short, medium and long-terms needs to be prepared. A transport corridor with links to population and industrial centers and the hinterland should become top priority. That itself will generate considerable economic activity. It then should be followed by other infrastructure creation for movement of goods and people. Instead of standalone initiative, the BCIM economic corridor must be linked to other corridors such as Silk Road, BIMSTEC, China-Southeast Asia, GMC, etc. further, it could also be linked to India-Myanmar-Thailand Highway that is under-way, the proposed Bangladesh-Bhutan-India-Nepal Economic Corridor, and to the planned rail links between India and Southeast Asian mainland in the future

CONCLUSION

Despite its existence for more than a decade and a half, the BCIM has failed to make progress partly because so far politico-security considerations loomed larger than economic. However, the rise of East Asia, rapidly growing intra-regional economic linkages and regional economic interdependence and integration are forcing countries to seize opportunities wherever they present rather than concerned too much about perceived security challenges. A large number of Regional Trading Agreements (RTAs) along with pan-East Asian comprehensive economic partnership efforts (such as RCEP) and what is called 'networked FDI' or the fast-strengthening of value chain within East Asia are setting off a new dynamic of its own, which is having profound impact on political relations. Despite enormous political fluidity, a lack of classic balance of power, numerous territorial disputes, uncertainty caused by the rise of new power centers, concerns about a viable regional security architecture, and occasional tensions among great powers, there is no denying that East Asia largely has been peaceful, politically stable and economically vibrant for more than three decades and half.

Insofar as regional economic dynamism is concerned, besides many other factors (including prominently market compulsions), sub-regional economic cooperative frameworks, for example, ASEAN, GMS, BIMSTEC, etc., are beginning to play a key role in driving the process of economic development and cooperation. Viewed in this light, BCIM has enormous potential to significantly play a larger role in bringing not merely the immediate regions that the proposed economic corridor is to be build but also a much larger region since it includes two fastest growing economies in the world with combined population of over 2.5 billion. A major shortcoming in realizing the BCIM's potential is poor infrastructure. If the connectivity is improved, the commerce will automatically take off. In this endeavor, India and China have a critical role to play. Now that the top political leadership is keenly pushing to create the BCIM corridor, it should be relatively easy to pursue it. Further, the BCIM can also linked to other sub-regional initiatives such as GMS, BIMSTEC and ASEAN.

REFERENCE

[1] 12th BCIM Forum for Regional Cooperation was held in February 2015 in Yangon but unfortunately hardly any details on outcome are available.

Implications of OBOR on Maritime Strategy and Security in the Indian Ocean

R. Sheshadri Vasan

ABSTRACT

The One Belt One Road (OBOR) initiative has caused ripples in Economic, Strategic, and Political spheres not just in the neighbouring countries but around the world. By design the OBOR will impact the entire world by the sheer scale and size of this mammoth project. The ingredients namely, opportunities for using the surplus fund, utilisation of surplus capacity and providing connectivity to find new markets are the success mantras for this century and beyond. Both the land and sea routes would provide China with opportunities for raising the bar in terms of becoming a super power

The declaration of the MSR in September 2013 by Xi Jinping opened up new vistas for expanding the foot print of China in the Indian Ocean and beyond to protect its sea borne interests while simultaneously providing leverages for increasing the influence in the target countries in South, South East Asia and Africa. The developing cash starved countries in India's maritime neighbourhood would welcome any investment on easy terms that would improve the livelihood and employment opportunities for its own citizens. From the Chinese point of view, it would have found new avenues in which to invest the surplus reserves expected to be in the region of three trillion by using AIIB and other banking sectors to facilitate the process. This will enable China to closely interact with the destination countries by employing its technology, manpower and pool of advisors/consultants.

The CPEC and the BCIM are the arteries that will carry goods through the Central Asian Republic states and through Bangladesh, India and Myanmar again opening up new vistas literally and figuratively. While the CPEC provides an exit to the Arabian Sea, the BCIM will provide an exit to the Bay of Bengal and will largely serve the interests of China which is looking for alternate routes for carriage of its energy needs as well as products to serve the markets of the world. The developments in Maldives have been worrisome for the Indian establishment and the Chinese are now moving in a big way with investments and assistance that will create bondage that would be difficult to ignore from the security point of view.

The OBOR is a game changer in the region and India obviously has serious concerns about the possible impact of the OBOR in its neighbourhood. Except some halfhearted effort on projects such as Mausam[1] or spice route, there is no concrete proposal to respond to the growing influence of China which will alter the strategic balance in the region. The paper seeks to examine the impact in all its dimensions and also offer some recommendations about possible India's responses.

MSR AND A HISTORICAL PERSPECTIVE

The new grand initiative under the leadership of Xi Jinping to connect the entire world both over the land routes and the sea routes has received mixed reactions and responses from its Asian neighbour India. The Maritime initiative with the nomenclature of Maritime Silk Road (MSR)[2] was announced nearly two years ago by a dynamic leader Xi Jinping.[3] The Chinese Government is committed to providing the necessary funds and assistance to build ports, harbours and related infrastructure in the destination countries in South East Asia, South Asia Africa and beyond. This doubtlessly is a very ambitious plan on a gigantic scale that would provide the necessary impetus to the economic growth and integration of the developing countries. The blue print is ready and the process has already been set in to motion. There are no doubts that this would immensely benefit both China and the recipient nations. From China's view point, it provides an opportunity for securing its sea borne interests far and wide as it seeks to sustain its economic success by seeking new avenues in far corners of the world. From the Chinese view point, it has been touted to be the harbinger of prosperity and a key to joint development.[4]

The initiative does remind one of the long and arduous journeys undertaken by Admiral Zheng He[5] during the rule of the Ming dynasty more than five centuries ago. The large fleet consisting of Junks, auxiliaries, supporting vessels and merchant ships sailed the oceans from South China Sea to the Indian Ocean and touched many ports in Asia and Africa establishing maritime trade relations. The ancient maritime silk routes carried the special commodity called 'silk' which was invented by the Chinese. Silk traveled both through the land routes and the sea routes to destinations around the world which was mesmerized by the silken quality of the cloth which was manufactured under a special process known only to the Chinese at that time. The markets and empires around the world would go to any length to procure this exquisite material and was used for bartering with China and to increase the prospect for trade in other commodities from the west. Trade has this unique quality of bringing both it with desirable and undesirable influences between the two trading countries and these would be discussed subsequently.

Right up to the seventeenth century, both China and India were rich nations who accounted for more than 40 percent of the global GDP. If it was silk that China concentrated on, India used the spice routes to transport the wonderful spices from the sub-continent to the rest of the world. This process also enabled the spread of the most vibrant Buddhist religion particularly to East Asia. The notable feature is that this spread of the religion was without the use of sword and it was mostly the appeal of this religion to the people of East and South East Asia that made it possible for Buddhism from the land of peace to spread far and wide notably to the east of India. While it is trade that enabled both China and India to reap rich dividends to achieve spectacular growth, it is the same trade routes that brought the East India Company to the shores of India purely for trade and commerce. As they say, it was only a matter of time before trade interests morphed in to the crown interests of Great Britain, traders became masters and India was brought under the yoke of the colonial masters. The advent of British in the 17th century also marked the down fall of both the Asian powers and both the countries had wait for this century for the renaissance and reinvention of the glorious past. It also may be noted that India was considered the Jewel of the British Crown as India was constantly plundered and the wealth transferred to Britain.

THE PRESENT CONNOTATION OF MSR

Coming back to the Maritime Silk Route and the Land Silk Route, it is clear that China which has sustained phenomenal growth rates and is the manufacturing hub of the world has long term strategy of protecting its overseas interest through the OBOR. The facts are easy to understand when the context and the emerging strategic contours are examined. China has the economic power and a leadership that knows how to use economy as leverage for promoting China's interest in the Asian century. Let us look at the maritime silk route in a little more detail. China today is a lead importer of energy goods from Middle East and Africa. All this has to pass through the Indian Ocean and also through the Choke points in Straits of

Hormuz and the Malacca Straits. The value of trade including energy products that pass through the South China Sea is of the order of three trillion USD. This amply demonstrates the criticality of maintaining safe corridors that allow the passage of such large volumes without external threats.

CHALLENGES IN THE MARITIME DOMAIN IN THE BACKDROP OF MSR

While no nation wants to go to war, today, all the maritime nations today are weary of non-state actors including Pirates who have threatened safe passages and the lives of seafarers by inducing in unlawful acts. Piracy peaked between 2005 and 2009 in the waters off the African Coast.[6] At one time, there were more than a thousand hostages in the custody of the Pirates raising concerns about the safety of merchant vessels and the seafarers. Commencing 2008, both India and China have maintained a continuous presence of their naval ships off Somalia and have even assisted each other in warding off threats to their vessels. The threat of piracy in the waters off Somalia has receded in the last few years as a result of the combined actions of the navies of the world and also the concerted action by the seafarers who implemented many onboard measures including carriage of the Privately Contracted Maritime Security Professionals (PCMSP) for transits through the High Risk Area (HRA). The HRA was declared taking in to consideration the pattern of attacks and likely areas in which the threat to shipping was expected. The unfortunate part is that the scene has shifted to the Malacca Straits and the South China Sea where more number of such attacks have been reported. Going by the report of both the Piracy Reporting Centre and the Re-CAAP this year, it is clear that the non-state actors are finding new methods to attack ships both at anchorage and also during transit from one port to the other. They are becoming more professional and using modern communication and navigation aids. They are also controlled by the handlers ashore who have access to the movement of ships by information such as the AIS and Vessel Tracker which are available to anyone who has the equipment.

What is the relevance of the above to the MSR and to India's concerns? The Maritime Silk Route is not a standalone project with only trade and economic interests in mind while primarily it is that. It is only a matter of time before more countries joined the MSR initiative. This would provide new ports that would come under the ambit of the International Ship and Port Security Code (ISPS). The overall security environment would be complimented with greater levels of security awareness and training among port operators, owners, managers and the crew.

SRI LANKA ISSUES

The case in example is the tilt of the Mahenda Rajapakse Government in Sri Lanka which heavily depended on Chinese investments post the military defeat of the LTTE. It also considered the strength of China with its Veto power that could help Sri Lanka to get out to tricky situations during the difficult periods when it was being pressurized to agree to a International tribunal for investigating the war crimes during the final phases of war in 2009. The post war period saw massive investments from the Chinese and India perceived the increased engagement in Sri Lanka as a challenge in its traditional neighbourhood.

The investments in Hambantota to develop this deep water port were interpreted as an attempt by China to seek a foot hold in the Indian Ocean Region. While the former President of Sri Lanka, Mahinda Rajapaksa publicly indicated that China is not interested in a naval base in Sri Lanka,[7] he favoured China for all investments in Sri Lankan mega projects. From the Chinese point of view, it is clear that

China which has a large share of it merchandise using the Indian Ocean was taking measures to protect its sea borne interests. However, what resulted was that Sri Lanka which historically had strong cultural, trade and security relations with India was seen as abandoning its century's old friendship. These doubts were also fired by the deployment of Chinese submarines from Colombo particularly on the eve of the visit of the President Xi Jinping to India. China has always been interested in the Indian Ocean due to both commercial and strategic reasons.[8] The deployment of the nuclear submarine in the Indian Ocean also brought in concerns about the intentions of the PLA Navy strategic assets in Bay of Bengal. While this may or may not be a deliberate action and not necessarily aimed at India, it was seen as an attempt to signal to the rest of the world including India that China now has the ability to operate in Indian Ocean to serve its own interests. It was also indicated that the Submarine was being deployed against piracy attacks. This again was interpreted as something that was not from the book of standard practices as the submarines are ineffective platforms against pirates. Indian leaders have clarified that every nation has a right to use the oceans of the world and China is no exception. However, it was the timing that appeared to send the wrong signal about the nature of such deployment of submarines. The change of leadership and the Government in Sri Lanka again has brought about some kind of balance that seeks to manage the sensitive relations with both the Asian Powers without displeasing either country. However, without the financial clout and also the supportive decision making process in India, it is at considerable disadvantage while thwarting the advances of China which is a past master at this game of enjoying other target nations through economics and diplomacy. It will be well-nigh impossible for India to compete with a 11 trillion dollar economy[9] that impacts all corners of the globe. It is clear that the One Belt One Road

will be a key component of the growth of China in the next
five year plan.[10] The outward investments are largely likely to
be driven by OBOR.[11]

MALDIVES

The case of Maldives again is something that is being viewed
with serious concern in India. India has been a strong
supporter of Maldives and even bailed out the Government of
Maumoon Abdul Gayoom in the late 80s from an imminent
take over from a mercenary group from Sri Lanka. The
operation Op Cactus was a spectacular success and ensured
that India and Maldives continued to cooperate. However,
again with the change of Government by the ouster of
President Mohamed Nasheed, things have changed for the
worse in terms of India-Maldives relations. The cancellation
of the airport contract was seen as a turning point along with
the change of Government that appeared to be favouring
China over India. The recent parliamentary agreement in
Maldives that allows China to own up to a value of 25 percent
of the GDP of Maldives was seen as specially aimed at
providing China with a foot hold in the Indian Ocean. India
cannot blame China for this development. However it may be
recalled that there is a tri-lateral treaty on defence and security
cooperation between India, Sri Lanka and Maldives which is
aimed at ensuring that the Maritime Domain Awareness
(MDA) in the region is augmented by cooperative and
collaborative action by the three nations that would assist
maritime safety and security. This needs to be used as leverage
for furthering the strategic relations with Maldives and Sri
Lanka.

GWADAR AND CPEC

The case of Gwadar, a sea port on the Makaran coast has a
different connotation as it is not only a port on the MSR but

also now has been put on the over the land route through the China-Pakistan Economic Corridor, another ambitious project that connects the port of Gwadar[12] now being managed by China through the Central Asian Republics and also notably through the Pakistan Occupied Kashmir. China has committed more than one billion US Dollars for providing road and rail connectivity to Gwadar from Western China. This is doubtlessly a bone of contention as India views this as totally avoidable, more so, when China has serious reservations about India's initiatives and off shore explorations with Vietnam in the disputed areas though India has been collaborating with Vietnam in exploration activities since 1988 through its commercial enterprise Oil Videsh Nigam which is owned and operated by the Oil and Natural Gas Commission of India. It is not difficult to understand the importance of Gwadar to Chinese strategic interests. Gwadar would provide the exit to the Arabian Sea close to the Straits of Hormuz through which the critical energy products exit for China. Also, it provides an alternate land route for the energy goods both for normal and contingent situations. So it is clear that Gwadar serves the long term need of China in terms of obtaining a foot hold in the Arabian Sea close to the Straits of Hormuz and also provides option for overseas transit of energy products through the CPEC. From the Indian view point, there is again a lot that needs to be done to get its act together as for as Chabahar is concerned. The Indian officials have maintained that this is a commercial venture[13] and there are no lanes for setting up of a naval base in this port. Despite a lot of initial enthusiasm, both India and Iran are yet to move forward to invest and improve this port which is just some 72 kilometers to the west of Gwadar.

While it is Gwadar that would open the gates to the Arabian Sea, the Bangladesh China India Myanmar (BCIM)[14] would provide the necessary connectivity (Transport, Telecommunication and Energy) to the region that requires all the attention, and it also provides an exit to the Bay of Bengal. There can be no doubts that it will bring prosperity and economic investments of a huge order to the nations that have great stakes in developing the region. From the Indian view point, it is almost like a pincer movement with one arm extending from over the land routes in to the Arabian Sea and the other one extending in to the Bay of Bengal.

As for as the MSR is concerned, even some of the South Eastern countries have not been enthusiastic about the MSR and have even expressed concerns that are in the public domain. The observations of the Indonesian official are noteworthy as it sums up the apprehensions of some of the South East Asians. Likewise, Philippines is not in the grand scheme of MSR due to the historical differences between the two nations and also possibly due to the fact that Philippines approached the International Court of Justice (ICJ) to settle the disputes in the South China Sea related to territorial claims.[15] China apparently has indicated that it is not excluding Philippines and Philippines is welcome to join the initiative.[16]

THE BIG PICTURE

The MSR in its final shape once it connects all the dots in the three continents can bring about greater coordination and cooperation amongst maritime nations and other stake holder. On completion, the MSR would have the components for multi-lateral cooperation and opportunity in an area that requires greater coordination in the maritime domain to combat peace time maritime challenges such as Anti-Piracy, Search and Rescue, Humanitarian Assistance and Disaster relief, combating Environmental pollution and such like. In an area prone to typhoons and cyclonic storms it would be a good idea to pool the resources and have a common agenda that brings the nations on the MSR together. The loss of MH

370 with many Chinese nationals[17] and the Air Asia aircraft in 2014 has exposed the gaps in the Search and Rescue architecture of the region. This needs to be addressed by having contingency plans that integrate the potential of the region and optimize the same to prevent recurrences of the MH 370 variety.

INDIA'S CONCERNS AND OPTIONS

From the point of view of India which was subjugated to colonial rule through the trade initiatives of a British company, it has bitter memories of trade being used by the British to serve the purpose of bringing India under its rule. India has a dominant position in the Indian Ocean thanks to Geography. Also, since 1971, its Navy has come of age and has become the most powerful regional navy[18] in the Indian Ocean. It has also been engaging its maritime neighbours and contributing effectively to stabilizing the maritime environment. In its perception, the active engagement of China with the traditional allies of India has to the potential to change the status quo.

India will continue to dither on whether to join in on the MSR initiative. There are serious concerns on how China will suffocate India with its huge economic investments in the Ports, related infrastructure, and hinterland connectivity in the destination countries. This in the assessment of India would gradually but steady increase China's capacity to wield influence in India's traditional neighbourhood. As a corollary, India fears an erosion of its own power to wield influence in its traditional back yard in the Indian Ocean. Officially, India has maintained that it would support the MSR initiative depending on the understanding of the proposals and schemes of China in the areas identified. However, it is clear that India would constantly be suspicious of the long term impact of China's presence in the Indian Ocean. That India has conceded substantial strategic space to China is not in doubt anymore. The actions of India are more akin to damage control.

India is not in a position to take a confrontationist stand against the initiatives of China as they are economically oriented and supported by robust funding through strong banking systems such as the AIIDB. The estimation of the ESCAP is that there would be a requirement of 800–900 billion dollars[19] annually in the region and the AIIDB would meet substantial requirement of this gigantic requirement of development. That substantial money has been earmarked and available for release to different projects identified in the MSR would encourage more nations along the planned MSR string to join the initiative. The expectation is that it would help both in the short and long term specifically in terms of economic engagement with China which is willing and capable of spending large sums of money. Some of the Chinese scholars have gone to the extent of labeling the MSR as stratified, orderly international trading system[20] with India, China, India and Europe as the core regions (First Class Regions).

India would not like to be seen as a silent spectator who is just allowed to watch the proceedings in its backyard. Despite the reservations that it has on the long term impact of MSR on the strategic landscape, India may have to ultimately show its support selectively to some of the projects in India. The signals being sent out by Delhi are that they are not rejecting the MSR but would like to know specific plans and proposals for consideration. There are both supporters and detractors of the MSR and the advantages have been shown to be much more than any kind of disadvantage particularly with the focus on developing economies of the region. These views have been well orchestrated by R. Chaudhary in the Economic Times[21] on 09 April 2015.

In this essay it has been suggested that "We should promote cooperation in the connectivity of energy infrastructure, work in concert to ensure the security of oil and gas pipelines and other transport routes, build cross-border power supply networks and power-transmission routes, and cooperate in regional power grid upgrading and transformation. We should jointly advance the construction of cross-border optical cables and other communications trunk line networks, improve international communications connectivity, and create an and create an Information Silk Road. We should build bilateral cross-border optical cable networks at a quicker pace, plan transcontinental submarine optical cable projects, and improve spatial (satellite) information passageways to expand information exchanges and cooperation."[22]

It would be in the interest of India to get in to a dialogue mode on where is it feasible for both China and India to work together in the region for both regional integration and prosperity. A proactive approach from India would be the need of the hour to use this challenge posed by China as an opportunity to get its own act together. India needs to ensure that it does not lose out by opting out of a project that will go ahead with or without India's participation.

CONCLUSION

There can be no doubts that the OBOR is a great initiative that would provide connectivity and opportunity for all the nations in the region to grow. The committed funding would ensure that the infrastructure and other related areas would enable the ports, cities, towns and villages to be on a road map development. That there would be strategic dividends and spin offs in the long run is undisputed. The over the land route that passes through Central Asian Republic will again change the way Asia would be economically integrated. The road to prosperity and progress as claimed by the China and also so perceived by many of the recipient countries will also impact the strategic contours of Asia both over land and Sea. The MSR as discussed will be a game changer not just for China which has a clearly defined agenda but also for the countries in the Indian Ocean Region. The country that appears most affected is India which due to both geographical advantage and also the traditional/historical linkages with the IOR littorals enjoyed a unique status. All that would now be subject to serious changes that will redefine China's role in the Indian Ocean Region. There are no doubts that China is here to stay as an Extra Regional Power in the IOR and will jostle for power and influence alongside India.

While the options are enormous and also the deliverables heavily loaded in favour of China, the leadership of China has even a greater role and responsibility to address the concerns of the nations and reassure them that there is only one agenda and that is of economic development and integration of Asia, Africa and even the West. That the long term benefits of MSR outweigh the perceived disadvantages if any needs to be brought out clearly to the partners of MSR. By addressing the concerns of countries in the region and getting more countries to endorse the MSR would ensure that the gate ways to prosperity are opened both over land and the sea routes.

India on its part also has to revisit the related issues of MSR and the Land routes. Its genuine concerns particularly about the connectivity through the Pakistan Occupied Kashmir (PoK) need to be addressed through dialogue as it has the potential to breed suspicion in the minds of the two growing Asian powers. It is not out of place to mention that there is hardly any issue of difference between China and India except the land borders which has remained a sore point in the relations. The speedy resolution to the land borders would ensure that the two Asian powers are able to put their differences behind them and work together to tackle global issues that challenge Asia. India is left in a position where it has no choice but to fire on all its cylinders to ensure that it is not left out in the race in which China is already in the Number One position and India is in a position where it cannot even take the second place for granted.

REFERENCES

[1] Touted to be the counter to the MSR, but not much seems to have taken off on the ground http://thediplomat.com/2014/09/project-mausam-indias-answer-to-chinas-maritime-silk-road/report on diplomat accessed on 03 Dec 2015. The website of IGNCA also has a mention of the project but has mostly cultural and historical projects associated with Mausam vide http://ignca.nic.in/mausam.htm accessed on same date.

[2] Maritime Silk Road issues highlighted during the speech of the Chinese Premier Xi Jinping on 02 October 2013 available http://www.asean-china-center.org/english/2013-10/03/c_1330 62675.htm accessed on 07 Jan 2016.

[3] The ambitious scheme was announced in 2013 in Indonesia and aims to connect the continents both by land and sea routes.

[4] Global Times had organized a forum in October 2014 and the views of different speakers reinforced the view that MSR is a tool for joint development of ASEAN and provide connectivity of the three continents http://www.globaltimes.cn/content/889599. shtml accessed on 05 Jan. 2016.

[5] Admiral Zheng sailed the oceans and travelled far and wide by visiting countries in South Asia, South East Asia and also countries in Africa in an expedition under the Ming dynasty. China also commemorated his journey by replicating the routes from South China Sea right up to African coast.

[6] Boon, Kristen E., Lovelace, Douglas C. (Jr.), Piracy and International Maritime Security: Developments through 2011, Vol. 125, Oxford Press 2012, pp. 194–197.

[7] Brewster, David, Indian Ocean Story of India's bid for Regional Leadership, Routledge, London 2014, p. 56.

[8] Holmes, James R., Winner, Andrew C., Yoshihara, Toshi, Indian Naval Strategy in the Twenty-first Century Routledge, 2014, pp. 128–48.

[9] In a commentary by Gordon Gorr carried by Mckensey and Company accessed on 06/01/2016 and available at http://www. mckinsey.com/Insights/Strategy/What_might_happen_in_China _in_2016?cid=other-eml-alt-mip-mck-oth-1601

[10] Ibid from Gordon's predictions for China in 2016.

[11] Ibid in assessment of how China will go global using the OBOR.

[12] Kirchberger, Sarah, Assessing China's Naval Power: Technological Innovation, Economic Constraints and Strategic Implications, Springer Heidelberg, New York 2015.

[13] Kemp, Geoffrey, The East Moves West: India, China, and Asia's Growing Presence in the Middle East, Brookings 2010, p. 168.

[14] Zheng, Dawei (Ed) Control, Mechatronics and Automation Technology: Proceedings of the IRAICS, Taylor and Francis London 2015, p. 485.

[15] As brought out in Wall Street Journal on 10th November 2014. http://www.wsj.com/articles/china-bypasses-philippines-in-its-pr oposed-maritime-silk-road-1415636066 accessed on 10th December 2015.

[16] http://www.philstar.com/headlines/2014/11/14/1391707/china-denies-excluding-philippines-maritime-silk-road Philippines Star web version accessed on 10th December 2015.

[17] Full details available in Wikipedia. https://en.wikipedia.org/wiki/ Malaysia_Airlines_Flight_370 accessed on 04 Jan 2016.

[18] Muhammad, Anwar, Friends Near Home: Pakistan's Strategic Security Options, Author House Bloomington, 2006, p. 45,

[19] Cho, Lee-Jay and Lee, Chang Jae, Financing Economic Integration and Functional Cooperation for Northeast Asia, North East Economic Forum Publication, 2014, p. 38.

[20] Wang, Rong, Zhu, Cuiping, Annual Report on the Development of the Indian Ocean Region (2015): 21st Century Maritime Silk Road, Springer, 2015, pp.132–135.

[21] http://economictimes.indiatimes.com/news/defence/indo-china-joint-silk-road-economic-belt-maritime-silk-road-china-seeks-to-address-misgivings/articleshow/46860971.cms accessed on 03, Dec. 2015.

[22] Ibid.

Sino-India Competition and Cooperation Protract as Parallels

Yagma Reddy

HISTORICAL GEOGRAPHY AT THE BASE OF SINO-INDIAN GLORIOUS PAST AND GLOOMY PRESENT

The geography-imposed-obstacles as well as the non-expansionist nature of the Indian civilization had virtually ruled out the chances of military clash between the two Asian giants for over thousands of years. Historically, the Sino-Indian border was not under dispute as Himalayas remained as a natural barrier[1] to military adventurism in either direction. They were thus oblivious of each other's existence for over a millennium until they began experiencing European influence from 19th century. During the previous 5000 years of recorded human history, save the last 300 years, it was India and China that dominated world trade and technology[2] Certainly, at the beginning of the beginning of the 18th century, China and India dominated the world not merely demographically, but also in terms of their economic strength as discernible in their contribution of 23.0 per cent and 22.6 per cent respectively to the world income.[3] If the 19th century witnessed China and India were losing their global preeminence, they fell behind in the first decades after World War II because of dogmatic precepts of communism by Mao Zedong, Chairman of the People's Republic of China, and the socialist leanings of Jawaharlal Nehru, the first Prime Minister of the Republic of India.[4]

India and China, representing world's two great civilizations, were known for resilience and prosperity for over 3000 years, even as the political contacts between them were far and wide. Absence of a border agreement between China and India historically led to no formal fixing of the boundary; and their border activities had been carried out on the basis of a traditional customary border. Evidently, there was no way to correctly measure the total length of the traditional customary border.[5] The Himalayan Ranges, though formed the territorial-divide, could not offer the scientific boundaries; yet, both the nations have given little credence to the logic of geography and legacy of history pertaining to the formidable Himalayan mountain system that thwarts human efforts at exercising an effective control over the borders. Yet, the Himalayas do not pose any fundamental barrier to military operations from Chinese-held Tibet against India, as vindicated by the Sino-Indian war of 1962, especially in an age of missiles and with China holding the heights.[6] The "protracted geopolitical conflict" in Sino-Indian relations for the last 50 years is reminiscent of a Cold War of its own.

DIVERGENCE OF TERRITORIAL CLAIMS BASED IN III—DRAWN BOUNDARY

The geographical exigencies of the formidable Himalayan mountain system that serve as a natural asset as well as a liability to either of these nation-states which have often been subjected to tensions all along the border that could be neither well-defined nor defended in view of the ground realities. India's partition in 1947 and Chinese occupation of Tibet in 1950 made them the vicinal nations as if to confront over the territorial limits. The length of Sino-Indian border has been variously mentioned as, for instance, 2520 miles (4,032 km), according to Malik J. Mohan[7] and 4,250 km according to an official document of India.[8] Though these figures are very much at variance with border length of 3380 km, they are, however, closer to the one referring to the Line of Actual Control (LAC), the effective border between India and China (4,057 km long) that traverses three areas of northern Indian states: western, middle and eastern.[9] *The Global Times* (affiliated to People's Daily group)described the extent of disputed territory as follows: Total area in dispute of about 125,000 sq. km. encompasses Eastern Sector—90,000 sq. km; Middle Sector—2, 000 sq. km; and Western Sector—33,000 sq. km. This disputed area (125,000 sq. km.) in yet another way is categorized into two distinct parts: (1) The Western Sector—Aksai Chin, located in the Ladakh area of north eastern Kashmir (lying beyond the Karakoram range and resting on the Kunlun mountain range), covering an area of about 37,250 sq. km—currently occupied by China. (2) The Eastern Sector—the Indian state of Arunachal Pradesh, which China calls South Tibet, covering an area of 83,743 sq. km— currently occupied by India. David Scott at the International Relations, Brunei University, termed the territorial dispute as the clearest point of divergence between the two countries, though the extent of the disputed area is found at variance with the other sources: India claims around 40,000 square kilometers of Chinese controlled territory (Aksai Chin) on the western flanks of the Himalayas; China claims around 92,000 square kilometers of Indian controlled territory (Arunachal Pradesh) on the eastern flanks.[10] Obviously, the ill-drawn boundary has been at the base of cross-border violations wittingly or unwittingly to the extent of disrupting the spirit of neighbourliness. The relations between the two Asian giants since the 1962 Sino-Indian border clashes were thus "marked by conflict, containment, mutual suspicion, distrust and rivalry".

Both these Asian giants have their security apparatus calibrated to the precepts of geographical causation. The two Asian powers, lamented Vijay Sakhuja (at the Indian Council of World Affairs in New Delhi), continue to "suffer from a trust deficit and are increasingly concerned about each other's strategic intent, particularly over their respective military developments across the Himalayas", including the "augmenttation of defense forces and military infrastructure along the border". The boundary dispute gains greater salience given the fact that China has resolved its boundary disputes with most of its neighbors, while its dispute with India remains unresolved.[11] 'China Threat' perceptions have been buttressed by its concerted efforts aimed at 'strategic encirclement of India'. China's direct control of Xinjiang is complemented by direct hold on Tibet since 1950. The India-China rivalry is particularly striking, featuring a heady mix of factors: border disputes, China-Pakistan relations, maritime competition, the India-US strategic partnership, allegations of support for insurgents (in both directions) and Chinese dams in the Mekong. As far as conventional wisdom is concerned, India and China are strategic rivals, engaged in what is perceived as a zero-sum game, competing to occupy a dominant position in Asia and the world order, through geo-political maneuvering and expansion of their political and economic footprint.[12]

SINO-INDIAN MARITIME RIVALRY TESTIFYING TO MUTUAL TRUST—DEFICIT

Giving credence to the geo-strategic implications is nothing but an inexorable geopolitical reading on the lines of territory-security-military alliances. China's maritime multilateralism with Indian Ocean littorals from mid-1980s, by way of regular incursions into the Indian Ocean region and naval deployments in the region, has the potential to translate into strategic partnership. Through its tacit bases built in the Indian Ocean—electronic surveillance installations in Myanmar, maritime infrastructure developments in Bangladesh (Chittagong) and Sri Lanka (Hambantota) as well as at the deep-sea port in Pakistan (at Gwadar) both for commercial and naval activities—China could emerge as a stakeholder in the Indian Ocean security architecture.[13] China's grand strategy intended to encircle India by befriending the Indian Ocean littorals, what is of late characterized by the 'string of pearls', does speak of China's "long memory". Beijing sees the opening of this alternative energy-supply route against the backdrop of maritime territorial disputes in the East and South China Seas. The Myanmar-China pipelines give China the chance to move into the Indian Ocean and present a new dynamic to Asia's great power games.

India has also been seeking to improve its infrastructure along her disputed northern border with China, facilitating future deployment of military power. China's military alliances and forward deployment of its naval assets would definitely prompt India to respond by way of seeking access to ports in Vietnam (Cam Ranh Bay), Taiwan (Kao-hsiung) and Japan.[14] The geo-economic compulsions of the New Econo-mic Order have added a maritime dimension to the Sino-Indian geopolitical rivalry. The maritime rivalry, likely to be intensified in the Indian and Pacific Oceans ostensibly to safeguard their respective sea lanes of commerce and com-munication, will likely to intensify their mutual distrust and tensions.[15] That both the countries are "encroaching upon each other's spheres of influence" is testified by the fact that China does not like India's role far beyond South Asia, although it plays lip service to the notion that India should be a major player in the regional affairs. About the same time, India's entry into ARF was endorsed by the United States and Singapore and not by China. Inquisitively, China considers Indian Ocean as its next frontier, albeit it is not at all a littoral state. China's policies and actions are termed pretentious, given the fact that it wants to have China-dominated uni-polar Asia and a multi-polar world order. It was for this reason that the US presence in the Asia-Pacific region is favoured by countries which are wary of China's initiative of Shangai Cooperation Organization, largely feared as China-led 'East Asia Co-prosperity Sphere', rather 'Sino-centric Asian order' and 'Marshall Plan of Asia'.

Any attempt to achieve strategic parity with China, is strongly resisted by China through its military, economic and diplomatic means. As well as its ambitions, China has its expressed concern at the country's neighbours, including India's tacit security partnerships in the Asia-Pacific region. China has been skeptical of India being drawn into a United States-led "anti-China alliance, as is learnt from *Qiushi (Seek Truth)*, China's Communist Party's official magazine and an influential journal that is circulated among its members.[16] If China is engrossed to develop a credible maritime force to deal with its 'Malacca dilemma', it is equally committed "to build a powerful navy that adapts to our military's historic mission in this new century." Evidently, "New Delhi's strategic geography", as Vijay Sakhuja, a Naval strategic analyst pointed out, "is predicated on long-range naval operations and the exerciseing of influence around the strategic choke points of the Straits of Hormuz, the Straits of Malacca and the Sunda Straits".[17] If the simultaneous emergence of India and China as Asian and global powers has made them to be sensitive to each other's interests and aspirations, these two continental-size economies and political entities are too big to contain each other or be contained by any other country.[18] Although both consciously downplay their differences, "the two may never be friends, but will not go to war and will not queer the pitch beyond a point".[19] Even as the China-India rapprochement sought to underplay their 'trust deficit' syndrome, a "balance of power game" between India and China is basically entwined with geo-political space surrounding.[20]

SINO-INDIAN FRATERNAL FRIENDSHIP
TO USHER IN ASIAN CENTURY

The Sino-Indian geopolitical setting is looked upon as a fundamental factor for understanding the twenty-first century which is turning out to be "the century of China and India".[21] The phrases frequently used in the recent times, 'rise of China' and 'rise of India' do testify to their prominence as potential centres of political power and economic strength and as Asian giants giving credence to the concepts of Asian Century and New Asia.[22] In effect, the concepts of 'China's Century' and 'India's Century' have been amalgamated giving rise to the talk of an 'Asian Century' with a thrust on the amity and cooperation between India and China.[23] While quoting the U.K-based *Guardian* newspaper as having referred to India and China as "non-identical conjoined twins, joined at the Himalayas", Niharika Chibber Joe of the Maureen and Mike Mansfield Foundation also floated the idea of "Chindia".[24] The Western media was more than ready to use the phrase 'China's/Chinese Century', and the Indian commentators and politicians promptly started to talk of 'India's Century'.

Some proponents anticipating Asian Century are quite optimistic of the bigger role of the two most populous countries in the world affairs. Deng Xiaoping told Rajiv Gandhi that "unless both India and China become well developed, there is no such thing as an Asian Century". The Chinese Premier Wen Jiabao, while recalling his earlier visit to India in April 2005, stated that the Sino-Indian strategic partnership reached a 'historical stage' and fondly hoped that their 'fraternal friendship' could usher in a 'true Asian Century'.[25] While referring to the India-China relations during his visit to India in November 2006, the Chinese President Hu Jintao termed the rise of these two countries as "central to not only a new Asian century but to a new world order". Hu further favoured 'win-win cooperation' between India and China for achieving mutual development which he linked to the realization of Asian Century.[26] Hu also called for strengthening China and India trade and business links in pursuit of realizing 21st century as Asian Century. Chinese President Xi Jinping in his article in *The Hindu* (17 September 2014) expressed confidence over the realization of Asian Century at an early date if China and India work together. Xi's optimism over the combination of the "world's factory" and the "world's back-office" to produce the most competitive production base and the most attractive consumer market.[27] gains credence from the fact that India's strength lies in IT and software engineering, management and financial services and China's proven expertise in hardware, manufacturing, construction and engineering.

Prospects of Economic Cooperation Vindicated

The Chinese Ambassador in India, Zhang Yan, drew attention to the fact that China has become a leading trading partner of India, and India ranked ninth among China's partners.[28] Of much significance are the potential prospects for trade and economic cooperation leading to the signing of a Most Favored Nation (MFN) agreement in 1984. As a corollary, the bilateral trade that eclipsed the Sino-Indian historic acrimony so much as the 'Hindi-Chini-Buy-Buy' phenolmenon is gaining currency. The bilateral trade has begun to witness phenomenal growth from a minuscule of US $ 0.27 billion in 1990 to $ 20 billion in 2005 (with a trade surplus of $ 1.75 billion in favour of India) and then to $ 30 billion in 2007. Bilateral trade reached the mark of $ 61.76 billion in 2010, an increase of 42.4 per cent from 2009; and it as then projected to get doubled by 2015,[29] notwithstanding the glaring India's trade deficit from $ 28 billion in 2010–11 to $ 35.0 billion in 2013–14 hitting the highest of $ 40.8 billion in 2012–13. Nataraj and Sekhani (2014) have also noted that China has its investment in India accumulated to $ 57.6 million, as opposed to India's investment in China of $ 44.2 million by December 2011.[30] Economic ties between the two countries, according to the Indian Commerce Ministry, have been growing at the annual rate of some 30 per cent, which may result in China replacing the United States as India's leading trading partner.[31] By becoming complementary to each other, the economies of these two Asian giants grow to the extent of benefitting the world. The emerging Asian

Century would also become profitable to the US, just as it got benefitted out of Western Europe's economic recovery after World War II.

The sustainable China-India's economic complementarity and China-Japan's trading partnership testify to their greater economic dominance in Asia and demographic preponderance over the world. Further, their membership in a multitude of regional frameworks has become conducive to increasing economic interdependence with commercial links and promoting regional prosperity. The impressive positive trends in their bilateral relations since late 1980s include: regular high level political interactions; and boundary demarcation-talks since 2003; and joint military exercises, including two 'anti-terror' exercises in 2007 and 2008.[32] The two sides at the August (2009) border talks in New Delhi favoured 'apolitical solution' to the boundary problems and for 'safeguarding the peace and calmness in the areas along the border'.[33]

Scope for Expanding the Areas of Cooperation

Though the border issues remain contentious, China and India are set to increase cooperation in trade, space exploration and civil nuclear energy.[34] Deepening mutual trust by strengthening strategic dialogue and enhancing political confidence as well as bringing more benefits to each other by expanding the areas of cooperation were the reasons cited by Chinese President Xi Jinping for enhanced bilateral relations, as evident from the "close coordination and cooperation on climate change, food security, energy security and other global issues and upheld the common interests of our two countries as well as the developing world as a whole". New Delhi has of late begun looking at BCIM as one of the stepping stones to integrate itself closely with the East Asian economies; and

China is furthermore fervent of BCIM as a means of engaging India. The BCIM Corridor, which is initially started as Kunming Initiative, is expected to encourage further interest by Chinese and Indian firms in Myanmar. The proposed 312 km stretch of Stilwell Road, which connects Northeast India with Yunnan through northern Myanmar, could lower transportation costs between India and China by 30 per cent, besides accelerating the Sino-Indian trade through the BCIM Corridor. The BCIM Corridor is devised to improve connectivity through the construction of the BCIM economic corridor, through railways, highways, personnel and informa-tion flows, tourism, energy links and people-to-people contact. This win-win arrangement, as Sahoo and Bhunia[35] observed, might well be the game changer that South Asia needs.

Besides the revival of the Northern Silk Road rather a 'Silk Road Economic Belt' for land connectivity initially with Central Asia, China in 2013 devised a '21st century Maritime Silk Road' to connect China with ASEAN and, ultimately, with the coastal cities of South Asia as well. This initiative, proposed by Chinese President Xi Jingping later in October 2013 is intended to realize China's dream of 'great rejuvenation of the Chinese nation'. But, on the face of it, Xi Jinping outlined the "need to jointly develop the BCIM Economic Corridor, discuss the initiatives of the Silk Road Economic Belt and the 21st Century Maritime Silk Road, and lead the sustainable growth of the Asian economy"[36] MSR is part of One Belt One Road initiative for expanding the footprint of China in the Indian Ocean and beyond to protect its sea borne interests and simultaneously providing leverages for increasing the influence in the countries of South Asia, Southeast Asia and Africa. MSR is also intended to open up economic opportunities in this vast region.

In June 2014, the Chinese Ambassador to New Delhi, Wei Wei, proposed the establishment of a 'Trans-Himalaya Economic Growth Region (THEGR)' to promote the interconnection and joint prosperity of China and India and neighbouring countries through establishing new economic corridors. Another would be establishing India–China connectivity through the Nathu La pass in Sikkim. Pradumna B. Rana of S. Rajaratnam School of International Studies, Nanyang Technological University, Singapore, in a recent study prepared for the Asian Development Bank (ADB), proposed four multimodal Trans-Himalayan Economic Corridors (THECs) as well as proposed the expansion of the BCIM project to cover all of the South Asia Sub-regional Economic Cooperation countries. THEGR and THECs, as[37] elaborated, would reduce distance between major Indian cities and inner China cities by more than half through land routes vis-à-vis sea route and would be more cost-effective for transportation of less bulky items in great demand.

That India and China cannot afford to ignore each other is amply testified by half-a-dozen high profile visits within two years, including Chinese President Xi Jinping's visit to India in September 2014, Indian Prime Minister Narendra Modi's visit to China in May 2015 and the first-ever visit of a Vice-President of China, Li Yuanchao, to India in November 2015. These two countries have different reasons to cooperate with each other, the central objective remains 'coexistence'.[38] The visit of Modi to China was significant in as much as the two sides signed a record 24 agreements covering railways, mining, outer space, earthquake science and engineering, tourism, sister-cities and establishment of consulates in Chengdu and Chennai. The candid, constructive and friendly conversations between Modi and his counterpart Li Keqiang covered "all issues, including those that trouble smooth development of our relations".[39]

IMPLEMENTS AND INHIBITIONS IN
SINO-INDIAN PARTNERSHIP

All said and done, there have been bureaucratic hassles impeding the people-to-people, industry-to-industry or sub-region-to-sub-region exchanges and collaborations. The advice of Talleyrand, Napoleon's famous foreign minister that "by no means show too much zeal" has been grossly ignored by the personalities at the helm who have been shaping Indian diplomacy for long. The limited educational interactions between the two countries, as Tansen Sen points out, is due to the reluctance of the Indian Ministry of Home Affairs to issue visas to Chinese students and instructors and the failure of the BCIM sub-regional collaborative initiative. To quote Tansen Sen further:

> There are contradictions between the India-China joint declarations about promoting people-to-people exchanges and the implementation of these measures. Intra-ministerial disagreements, mystifying constraints, narrow visions and a reluctance to involve competent people often render these processes ineffective. These initiatives are usually categorised as 'public diplomacy' and epito-mised by heavy handedness and restrictions imposed by bureaucrats who treat them as no more than symbolic gestures. In fact, free interactions at the grassroots levels—that could potentially advance mutual awareness and knowledge—have never been fully encouraged seemingly for 'security' reasons. Consequently, the rhetoric and false narratives of friendship get recycled while the general public remain in the dark and utterly confused about the actual policy goals.[40]

Even as the rapprochement in the bilateral relations between China and India being variously viewed, Sino-Indian ties remain weak and vulnerable to sudden deterioration as a result of misperceptions, expectations, accidents and eruption of unresolved issues. The simultaneous rise of both China and India are bound to result in realignment of geographical equation and power relations in Asia. Further, the competetion for resources, overlapping spheres of influence, and rival alliance relationships would characterize the future relations between the two Asian giants more by competition than cooperation in the foreseeable future.[41] These are two powers, with common borders, each their own vulnerabilities, inexorably growing economic complementary, shared interests and objectives in global governance and the need to deal with each other's growing power in its own Asian space.[42] India's ties with China are thus gradually becoming competitive, with a sentiment gaining ground among Indian policy elites that China is not sensitive to India's core security interests and does not acknowledge its status as a global player.[43] Engaging with China bilaterally is an imperative for India, not an option.

NEED FOR RECONCILING TO EXPEDIENCY

With the collapse of the bipolar system, regional heavyweights such as India and China seek to attain regional hegemony, gradually expanding their "areas of interest" until they overlap, bringing about conflict. In the face of potential prospects, Sino-Indian rivalry is discernible in the existence of competing projects for regional cooperation, which mutually tend to exclude or diminish each other's presence, such as the Kunming Initiative or the Mekong-Ganga Cooperation Project. It is due to this complex nature of Sino-India relations that it cannot be explained in simplistic format of 'friend' and 'foe'. Instead, both constitute a mosaic of cooperation, co-existence, coordination, cooption, competition and even confrontation.[44] Sino-Indian collaborative scenario for the future is far from convincing, given their conflicting interests in their neighboring regions and their rivalry within the varied regional organizations in Asia. The massive Chinese investment in many of the littoral states in the India's neighbourhood attracted apprehension among the Indian policy makers in terms of challenges and threats to India's commercial, economic and political interest. Some of the Indian scholars argue on the lines of settling the Sino-Indian border dispute much before India joining the MSR initiative. But the border issue that defied the precepts of 4 Ds (Definition, Delineation, Demarcation and Defense) cannot be resolved instantly. The Sino-Indian border dispute remains as a test for China without entertaining adventurous hopes to challenge India's sovereignty.

India has since 2013 been reluctant to endorse the China's OBOR initiative, of which MSR is one part. Geethanjali Nataraj, a senior fellow at the Observer Research Foundation, New Delhi, opines that "if the maximum number of countries recognizes the benefits of OBOR, it will also strengthen China's economic and political positioning. More than anything, if India refuses to be part of the Silk Road and the rest of the South Asian and ASEAN countries decide to join then India may become isolated. In this situation, it would be best for India to accept the invitation to join the MSR while availing itself every opportunity to join the US-led TPP".[45] India needs to bear in mind that China wouldn't lose anything on account of India remaining outside the framework of MSR.

Need for Reciprocity and Rapprochement

Building mutual confidence through disengagement and relocation of troops as well as reduction of tensions in the border areas would avoid uncalled for military confrontations. Policy makers, strategic analysts, and other think-tanks of both these nations are quite aware that a war between these nations would drain their resources and thwart the anticipated global power shift. India cannot afford to have a hostile and resentful China on its borders, nor could it gain any substance by entering into an anti-China alliance. Time has come for India and China to overcome differences and improve bilateral trade and economic relations. Although the misperceptions, distrust, suspicion and hostility towards each other would not instantly vanish, China and India should look to the future in building a relationship of friendship and trust based on equality in which each is sensitive to concerns and aspirations of others; this pace of increase in Sino-Indian trade is expected to continue. The maintenance and enhancement of the mutually beneficial, reciprocal and cooperative relations between China and India, as viewed by Ying.[46] are of great significance to their own development as well as to the regional stability and world peace, development and cooperation. The centre piece of the co-development strategy is the BCIM corridor; and it is fondly hoped to improve connectivity through the construction of the BCIM economic corridor, through railways, highways, personnel and information flows, tourism, energy links and people-to-people contact. Furthermore, both China and India have membership in as many as 4 Asian regional organizations (ARF, JACIK, EAS, RIC and BCIM) and BRICS as well as have the benefit of observer status in some other organizations (China in SAARC and India in SCO). Instead of being ridden with the geopolitical syndrome, these two Asian giants shall as well subscribe to the principle of rapprochement that would underplay the continuing rivalry and promote the much needed cooperation on win-win-strategy.

REFERENCES

[1] Adityatiwathia, "Balancer Needed in Asia", *The World Affairs Blog Network*, 6 July 2009.

[2] Athale, Anil A., "How India, China can mastermind the Asian Century", *Rediff.com India News*, January 05, 2010 (Accessed 11 August 2011).

[3] *Knowledge@Wharton,* "The Coming of the Asian Century: Reflections on China and India", 21 November 2005; Available at: http://knowledge. wharton. upenn. edu/article.cfm? articleid =1268 (Accessed 22 February 2013).

[4] *Glassvisage.hubpages.com,* "The Asian Century: The Role of the Orient in Today's Business", *Glassvisage.hubpages.com* (Accessed 11August 2011).

[5] Rajan, D.S., "Aksai Chin, Arunachal ours, says China", *South Asia Analysis Group*, Paper No. 1387, 20 May 2005.

[6] Vatikiotis, M., "India and China: A Delicate Dance", *International Herald Tribune,* 23 January 2006.

[7] Mohan, Malik J., "India-China Relations", *Berkshire Encyclopedia of China*, Berkshire Publishing Co., 2009: Available at: http:// www.apcss.org/core/BIOS/malik/india-china_relations.pdf (Accessed 8 August 2014).

[8] *Bharat Rakshak*; Available at: www.bharat.rakshak.com/LAND-FORCES/..../1962 chapter01. pdf (Accessed 6 August 2012).

[9] Rajan, D.S., "Aksai Chin, Arunachal ours, says China", *South Asia Analysis Group*, Paper No. 1387, 20 May 2005.

Rehman, Iskander, "Keeping the Dragon at Bay: India's Counter-Containment of China in Asia", *Asian Security,* 5 (2), 2009.

Rehman, Iskander, "Sino-Indian Border Skirmishes towards a Limited Confrontation", *IPCS Issue Brief,* No 117, September 2009a.

[10] Scott, David, "The Great Power 'Great Game' between India and China: The Logic of Geography", *Geopolitics*, Vol. 13, No. 1, 2008.

[11] Sakhuja, Vijay, "Maritime Multilateralism: China's Strategy for the Indian Ocean", *China Brief,* Vol. 9, Issue 22, 4 November 2009.

[12] Poonawalla, Shehzad, "*China is moving away from co-operation to confrontation*", *Rediff.com,* 13 May 2015; Available at: http:// www.rediff.com/news/column/china-is-moving-away-from-co-opera tion-to-confrontation/20150513.htm (Accessed 5 June 2015).

[13] Mohan, Malik J., "India-China Relations", *Berkshire Encyclopedia of China*, Berkshire Publishing Co., 2009: Available at: http:// www.apcss.org/core/BIOS/malik/india-china_relations.pdf Accessed 8 August 2014).

Rechard, B., "The Karakorum Highway: Opportunities and Threats", *Peace & Conflict*, 9/9, 2006.

[14] Mohan, Malik J., "India-China Relations", *Berkshire Encyclopedia of China*, Berkshire Publishing Co., 2009: Available at: http://www.apcss.org/core/BIOS/malik/india-china_relations.pdf (Accessed 8 August 2014).

[15] Mohan, Malik J., "India-China Relations", *Berkshire Encyclopedia of China*, Berkshire Publishing Co., 2009: Available at: http://www.apcss.org/core/BIOS/malik/india-china_relations.pdf (Accessed 8 August 2014).

[16] Krishnan, Ananth, "China's Communist Party sees India as part of U.S. "containment" strategy", *The Hindu*, 12 February 2011; Available at: http://www.hindu.com/2011/02/12/stories/20110 21266651900.htm (Accessed 21 April 2013).

[17] Sakhuja, Vijay, "Indian Navy: Keeping Pace with Emerging Challenges," in Lawrence W. Prabhakar, Joshua H. Ho and Sam Bateman, (eds.), *The Evolving Balance of Power in the Asia-Pacific: Maritime Doctrines and Nuclear Weapons at Sea*, Institute of Defence and Strategic Studies, Singapore, 2006.

[18] Saran, S., *Present Dimensions of the Indian Foreign Policy*; Available at: http://www.indianembassy.org/newsite/press_release/2006/Jan/2.asp (Accessed 27 September 2006).

[19] Ved, Mahendra, "India, China need to cook up a win-win deal", *Newstraitstimes*, 19 April 2010.

[20] Kumar, A., "A New Balance of Power Game in the Indian Ocean. India Gears up to Tackle Chinese Influence in Maldives and Sri Lanka", *Strategic Comments* (IDSA), 24 November 2006.

[21] Zou, Hanru, "The Century of China and India?" *China Daily*, 28 October 2005.

[22] Monarch, Barleen and Ding, Zhitao, "Asian Tigers, Hear them Roar", *Beijing Review*, 7, 10–13 April 2005.

[23] Balakrishnan, Paran, 'India Joins the Asian Century', *Rediff.com*, 3 January 2004; Available at: http://www.rediff.com/money/2004/jan/03guest.htm (Accessed 13 September 2013).

Scott, MacDonald, "The Asian Century is only delayed", *Asia Times*, 24 November 2004.

Lal, Rashmee, "Asian Century: West is Watching", *The Times of India*, 12 April 2005.

[24] Joe, Niharika Chibber, *Fifty Years of Sino-Indian Relations: The Idea of "Chindia"*; Available at: http://www.mansfieldfdn.org/pubs/commentary/niharika011006.htm (Accessed 26 July 2013).

[25] *Press Trust of India*, 'China, India can usher in a true Asian century', *expressindia.com*, 14 March 2006: Available at: http://www.expressindia.com/news/fullstory.php?newsid=64360 (Accessed 17 June 2012).

[26] IANS, "Rising China, India key to true Asian Century: Hu", 22 November, 2006: Available at: http://www.ians.Rising_China_India_key_to_true_Asian_century_Hu-nid-33987.html (Accessed 17 October 2012).

[27] *The bricspost.com*, China, India must usher in Asian Century: Xi, 17 September 2014; Available at: http://thebricspost.com/china-india-must-usher-in-asian-century-xi/#VJ_lN6soKA (Accessed 8 November 2014).

[28] Yan, Zhang, "India-China Economic Relations and Performance in the 21st Century"; Available at: http://www.isria.com/free/29_March_2011_21.php (Accessed 11 August 2011).

[29] *The Times of India* 2008, as quoted in Mohan, Malik J., "India-China Relations", *Berkshire Encyclopedia of China*, Berkshire Publishing Co., 2009.

[30] Nataraj, Geethanjali and Sekhani, Richa, "Border issues gnaw at stronger India-China trade ties", *East Asia Forum*, 3 October 2014; Available at: at http://www.eastasiaforum.org/2014/10/03/border-issues-negate-stronger-india-china-trade-ties (Accessed 4 June 2015).

[31] *Glassvisage.hubpages.com*, "The Asian Century: The Role of the Orient in Today's Business", *Glassvisage.hubpages.com* (Accessed 11 August 2011).

[32] Sakhuja, Vijay, "Maritime Multilateralism: China's Strategy for the Indian Ocean", *China Brief*, Vol. 9, Issue 22, 4 November 2009.

[33] *Xinhua News Agency*, 6 August 2009.

[34] Nataraj, Geethanjali and Sekhani, Richa, "Border issues gnaw at stronger India-China trade ties", *East Asia Forum*, 3 October 2014; Available at: at http://www. eastasiaforum.org/2014/10/03/border-issues-negate-stronger-india-china-trade-ties (Accessed 4 June 2015).

[35] Sahoo, Pravakar and Bhunia, Abhirup, "BCIM Corridor a game changer for South Asian trade", East Asia Forum.org, 18th July, 2014, Available at: http://www.eastasiaforum.org/2014/07/18/bcim-corridor-a-game-changer-for-south-asian-trade (Accessed 28 June 2015).

[36] *The bricspost.com*, China, India must usher in Asian Century: Xi, 17 September 2014; Available at: http://thebricspost.com/china-india-must-usher-in-asian-century-xi/#VJ_lN6soKA (Accessed 8 November 2014).

[37] Rana, Pradumna B., "Building Silk Roads for the 21st century", *East Asia Forum*, Available at: http://www.eastasiaforum.org/2014/08/16/building-silk-roads-for-the-21st-century (Accessed 8 June 2015).

[38] Hashmi, Sana, "Building the basis for India-China cooperation", *East Asia Forum*, 25 November 2015, http://www.eastasiaforum.org/2015/11/25/building-the-basis-for-india-china-cooperation/

[39] *The Indian Express*, 15 May 2015; Available at: http://m.newshunt.com/india/english-newspapers/the-new-indian-express/national/modi-tells-china-to-reconsider-its-approach-on-some-issues_39615242/996/c-in-l-english-n-newexpress-ncat-National (Accessed 25 September 2015).

[40] Sen, Tansen, India and China must think outside the 'bureaucratic box', *East Asia Forum*, 13 September 2014, Available at: http://www.eastasiaforum.org/2014/09/13/india-and-china-must-think-outside-the-bureaucratic-box (Accessed 8 May 2015).

[41] Gojree, Mehraj Uddin, "India and China: Prospects and Challenges", *International Research Journal of Social Sciences*, vol. 2(8), August 2013.

[42] Drysdale, Peter, 'China and India and the transition of regional power', *East Asia Forum*, 17 January 2011; Available at: http://www.eastasiaforum.org/2011/01/17/china-and-india-and-the-transition-of-regional-power-2/ (Accessed 19 October 2013).

[43] Pant, Harsh V., "Can China and India get along? Very unlikely", *Rediff.com*, 22 November 2012, Available at: http://www.rediff.com/news/slide-show/slide-show-1-can-china-and-india-get-along-very-unlikely/20121122.htm (Accessed 14 August 2013).

[44] Singh, Swaran, Haenle Paul and Saalman Lora, *China-India Relations: Friends or Foes?* Carnegie Endowment for Global Peace, Beijing, 2010.

[45] Nataraj, Geetanjali, "India should get on board China's Maritime Silk Road", *East Asia Forum*, 27 June 2015: Available at: http://www.eastasiaforum.org/2015/06/27/india-should-get-on-bo ard-chinas-maritime-silk-road/?p=46647 (Accessed 14 August 2015).

[46] Ying, Rong, *China-India Relations: New Starting Point and New Framework*, China Institute of International Studies, 10 August 2011; Available at: http://www.ciis.org.cn/english/2011-08/10/ content_4395790.htm (Accessed 20 December 2013).

China's Recent Policies Denting India's Interests: Economic and Security Concerns

R. Sidda Goud and Manisha Mookherjee

While China has been important to the world economy for decades, being world's second largest economy, it is now wielding its financial heft with the confidence and purpose of a global superpower. It represents a new phase in China's evolution, as Beijing surges forward and displaces the U.S. and Europe as the leading financial power in large parts of the developing world. With the Centre of financial gravity shifting, China is aggressively asserting its economic clout to win diplomatic allies, invest its vast wealth, promote its currency and secure much needed natural resources around the world.

China's rapidly expanding foot prints speaks volumes about the changing world order, as it represents a new phase in China's evolution with President Xi Jinping making major changes to its policies, domestic and foreign. This has been particularly evident in the foreign policy sphere with the new initiatives like the Foreign Aid Policies, the 'One Belt One Road' (OBOR) programme, spearheading the BRICS Development Bank, the Asian Infrastructure Investment Bank (AIIB)—symbolizing China's growing influence in development finance and Devaluation of its currency. These initiatives are aimed to expand China's business and to sell its excess capacity in manufacturing sector to Central Asian, South Asia, East Asia, Africa, West Asia/Middle East, Latin

America and Indian Ocean countries, through various corridors that China initiated under One Belt one Road (OBOR) programme. Under this OBOR programme, China plans to build a land based Silk Road Economic Belt and a 21st Century Maritime Silk Road. According to Zhang Wang, it is China's 'alternative diplomacy'. President Xi Jinping's strategy is a sophisticated and progressive one, wherein the Chinese are trying to create new platforms that Beijing can control or substantially influence. Through these new initiatives Beijing aims to create a new international environment that is more favourable to China, one that will limit strategic pressures from the U.S. These steps aim only to further economic development enterprises, and Beijing is trying to promote them as pure economic and trade initiatives. In the hind however, Beijing is trying to work for China's greater security and long term strategic objectives.[1] Therefore, these new initiatives of Aid Policies, OBOR and Devaluation of Currency are adversely impacting India in terms of economic, trade, political/geo-political and security concerns at a greater level. This paper attempts to analyse the adverse impact on India's economic policies and security concerns.

ECONOMIC HISTORY

Since the introduction of economic reforms in 1978, China experienced astonishing growth in the last few decades to become the world's second largest economy. It ranked 9th in nominal gross domestic product with USD of 214 billion and 35 years later—today it jumped to second place with 9.2 trillion USD.[2] The country to overcome backwardness decided to shift base into a hardcore capitalist economy from a communist socialist society with a high growth rate of 10.6 percent in 2010. Till the time of Mao Zedong's death in 1976, China was more backward than India, it was Den Xiaoping—the second generation of Chinese leadership who pushed bold reforms that reshaped the country's economy with the introduction of market driven mechanisms and reduced government control over the economy, which fetched high growth rate in the world. In the early 1990's Jiang Zemin, the third generation of Chinese leadership expanded the role of private sector in the economy and joined the World Trade Organization in December 2011, which enhanced the country's trade. In 2002, President Hu Jintao led the fourth generation of leadership who promoted social welfare by reducing the income gap between rural and urban areas. Finally in 2012, when President Xi Jinping came to power to lead the fifth generation of Chinese leadership, he unveiled an ambitious reform agenda from capital economy to market economy with high growth rate in the world. But however the Chinese economy has been struggling ever since from high debts and languishing exports and its continuous current slowdown in its economic growth rate since 2011 after a growth rate of 10.6% in 2010; 9.5% in 2011; 7.8% in 2012; 7.7% in 2013; 7.4% in 2014; and 6.9% in 2015 respectively. According to a Bloomberg survey it is expected to fall further in 2016 as the economy shifted base from export oriented to domestic consumption economy.[3]

FOREIGN AID POLICIES AND INVESTMENTS DENTING INDIA'S TRADE

China has the capacity to engage in substantial programmes of economic assistance and government sponsored investments in 93 emerging—market economics of the developing world, in six regions: Africa, Latin America, Middle East, South Asia, Central Asia and East Asia. In general China's use of foreign aid and government sponsored investment activities has burgeoned in recent years with emphasis on building infra-structure and supplies of natural resources, especially energy related resources, to fuel its falling economic growth rate to a 'New Normal' level. Therefore much of China's foreign aid has sought to expand supplies of such resources. In the first half of the 21ˢᵗ Century, China has expanded and directed this capacity in these countries for both their benefit and for China's own benefit as well. China's overseas finance is becoming increasingly influential globally. Between 2004 and 2013, China's overseas investments increased 13.7 times from 45 billion USD to 613 billion USD.[4] According to Charles Wolf Jr. *et al.*, 'the newly pledged aid from China was 124.8 billion USD in 2009, 168.6 billion USD in 2010, and 189.3 billion USD in 2011—all far above the 1.7 billion USD it pledged in 2001'.[5]

Apart from this, China has also extended aid to eight South Pacific Island countries with a view to control and influence the Pacific Ocean and on its resources. Between 2006 to 2011 China provided US $ 850 mn in bilateral aid to the eight countries (the Cook Islands, Federated States of Micronesia (FSM), Fiji, Niue, Papua New Guinea (PNG), Samoa, Tonga and Vanuatu) in the South Pacific with which it has diplomatic relations. Chinese aid is much visible and highly valued for its responsiveness, flexibility and focus on priority projects and sectors. Chinese aid helps these countries to build their much needed infrastructure. Since 2006 till 2014 China has given aid to the tune of US $ 1.479 bn in 169 projects across the South Pacific so as to grow its influence in the South Pacific region.[6]

AID POLICY DENTING INDIA'S EXPORT

The stipulations increasingly being made by China while extending financial aid to several developing economies is to buy medicines produced by their manufacturers, which have of late begun denting the exports of Indian drugs to these countries. According to Ministry of Commerce Government of India, currently exports around $ 15 billion worth medicines and the stipulations of China are affecting India's drug exports in the markets of Africa, Asia and Eastern Europe. China has been steadily accelerating aid to several developing economies towards capacity building in infrastructure, goods, materials, technical, human resources, agriculture, medical and health sectors. As against the $ 10 billion assistance extended between 2009 and 2012, Chinese President Xi Jinping announced doubling the aid to $ 20 billion during 2013–15. Adversely impacting India in terms of economic, political/geo-political and security concerns at a greater level.[7]

The impact of this enhanced financial aid amount and the Chinese stringent stipulation, Table 1 clearly indicates the declining trend of India's export in all the countries. According to P.V. Appaji, the Director General of Indian Pharmaceuticals Exports Promotion Council (Pharmexcil), nearly 140 million USD worth of Indian exports in the Pharmaceuticals industry was damaged by China during the year

Table 1: Dragon Denting India's Drug Exports

Sl. No.	Country	Exports in*	
		2013–14	*2014–15*
1.	South Africa	561	508
2.	Ethiopia	146	124
3.	Bangladesh	158	138
4.	Ukraine	115	86
5.	Sudan	81	79
6.	Kazakhstan	59	58
7.	Syria	30	20
8.	Tajikistan	19	14
9.	Belarus	16	15
10.	Angola	64	62

*Figures are in US $ Million.
Source: Pharmaceuticals Export Promotion Council of India, 2013–14, 2014–15.

2014–15. China has been increasingly insisting on several African, East European and a few Asian countries to buy its medicine while extending financial aid. As a result, there has been a dent in Indian drug exports to these countries (see table-1) wherein from 2013–14 to 2014–15 India's export value are steadily decreasing in all the countries. The Director General of Pharmexcil, Appaji, advised the Indian drug manufacturers to take note of this and accordingly sharpen their strategies for these markets to regain the lost ground and improve market shares.[8]

At present, China is the third largest pharmaceutical market with over $ 100 billion size, striving to narrow the gap with its rivals, US and Japan, the two top players with a size of $ 300 billion and $ 110 billion, respectively. As part of its efforts, China, the world's largest player in Active Pharmaceutical Ingredients (APIs), or raw material that goes into medicines, has stepped up investments in pharmaceutical formulations or finished medicine dosages.

MORE CHINA INVESTMENTS SOUGHT

To offset the impact of trade deficit, India had sought more investments from China especially in mega industrial parks (in States such as Gujarat and Maharashtra) so that products including electronic items, power equipment, footwear, industrial machinery, active pharmaceutical ingredients and apparel in addition to several value-added products can be manufactured in those parks and then shipped to China and other overseas markets. That way, India could increase its exports and simultaneously reduce the trade deficit with China. But, huge Chinese investments are yet to happen. In November, 2015 the Indian Union Minister for Commerce and Industry, Nirmala Sitharaman, during a meeting of the Parliamentary Consultative Committee (attached to the Ministry of Commerce & Industry), had voiced concern over

China "making efforts to stall" India's shipments to that country.

China, is continuing to stall India's exports using non-tariff barriers such as phytosanitary stipulations and standardisation measures. This is despite India laying emphasis on sectors such as IT/ITeS, pharma, textiles, gems and jewellery, fruits and vegetables and meat to increase the country's exports. India had taken up with China, during bilateral meetings and at the G-20, the issue of the widening trade deficit between India and China but the Chinese government only accepted India's concerns and had not taken action on them.

CHINA'S DEVALUATION OF CURRENCY—YUAN

While the devaluation is aimed at boosting China's exports, it is expected to have a direct impact on economies competing with China on that front. While the United States and the United Kingdom have started recovering, the turmoil in the Eurozone and weak global demand have shaken the Asian model of export-oriented growth. While India is already struggling on the domestic front with legacy issues like infrastructure and stalling of key legislations such as Land A question Bill and Goods and Services Tax (GST) Bill, a loss in currency competitiveness against the Yuan will further hurt its ailing exports.

China stunned the world's financial markets by continuously devaluing the Yuan for the second time, leading to over 4 per cent drop in its currency in two days. The devaluation of the Yuan strengthened the US dollar, while most other currencies were reeling for cover. The Indian rupee sank to a two-year low of 64.95 per dollar and, domestic stock market also came under selling pressure. The rapid drop in the value of China's currency—dealt a blow to the appetite for risky assets, and markets across the region plunged amid concerns that China has embarked on a damaging currency war. According to the

Assocham 'for India, the devaluation in the Yuan will prove to be a "triple whammy', firstly rupee volatility secondly, exports under pressure and thirdly, dumping of Chinese goods.

RUPEE VOLATILITY

The sharp fall in the rupee has already rattled stock markets, which fell for a fourth straight session today. If the rupee continues to fall sharply, imports will become costlier, stoking inflation. This will for the Reserve Bank to hold on to high interest rates, which will hamper the ongoing economic recovery. Since India runs a trade deficit (imports are more than exports), chances are the current account deficit will also rise, which will further pressure the rupee. Falling rupee is bad for those companies that have dollar-denominated loans and also for foreign flows because stock market returns become unattractive.

PRESSURE ON EXPORTS AND DUMPING
OF CHINESE GOODS

In normal course, falling rupee would have aided domestic exports, which have contracted for seven straight months until June 2015. However, analysts are betting against a rise in domestic exports because of a global slowdown. The face that China and India compete for several exports items such as textiles, gems and jewellery, etc., will also go against domestic exports. "The large overlap between Indian and China in markets and also products highlights the threat Indian exports face from China," said DK Pant, chief economist of India Ratings and Research. The economic slowdown in China— which is among the top five countries for Indian exports—is another negative for Indian exporters. There's fear that the devaluation in Yuan trice in a short span will help China dump goods into the Indian market, which will impact domestic manufacturers. The fear is already playing out on the

Dalal Street with tyre stocks and steel markers falling sharply over the last two days.

The decline in the value of China's currency against the dollar is a worrying development as it may lead to a sharp increase in cheap imports hurting several Indian industries. The depreciation of the Yuan may expand the country's trade deficit. "There is the issue of excess capacity in China leading to dumping and the apprehension that products will become even cheaper due to the currency devaluation because of what has happened now is the third major devaluation. There is also the fear that subsidized imports are coming in. These are worrying developments. India's trade deficit with China will grow even more.

India's merchandise trade deficit with China had ballooned from a minuscule $ 1.1 billion in 2003–04 to a whopping $ 48.5 billion in 2014–15 or over four times India's exports to China ($ 11.9 billion) in FY'15. During April-September this fiscal year, imports from China already touched $ 31.6 billion while India's exports to that country were only $ 4.5 billion, leaving a trade deficit of $ 27.1 billion.[8]

However, cumulative FDI inflows from China into India during April 2000–September 2015 were only $ 1.2 billion (or just 0.47 per cent of the total $ 265 billion worth overall FDI inflows into India in those 15 years), much less than the actual potential. There are reports of excess capacity in China, especially in sectors such as steel, leading to alleged instances of dumping of such products in several countries, including India, at rates below those in China or even lower than the production cost.[9]

CURRENCY DEVALUATION IMPACT ON INDIA'S TRADE

India and China officially resumed trade in 1978. In 1984, the two sides signed the Most Favoured Nation Agreement.

India-China bilateral trade, which was as low as $ 2.9 billion in 2000–01, reached $ 72.3 billion in 2014–15 (exports: $ 11.9 billion and imports: $ 60.4 billion), making China India's largest goods trading partner. But, India's trade deficit with China has almost doubled from $ 25 billion in 2008–09 to $ 50 billion in 2014–15, and China's share of India's total trade deficit is up from just under 20% in 2009–10 to 35% in 2014–15.[10] This is on account of rising imports coupled with weak export dynamics.

In a joint statement recently announced between India and China during Prime Minister Narendra Modi's visit to China in May 2015, it was agreed that both sides will take necessary measures to remove impediments to bilateral trade and optimally exploit the present and potential complementarities in identified sectors, including Indian pharmaceuticals, Indian IT services, tourism, textiles and agro-products. The two sides resolved to take joint measures to alleviate the skewed bilateral trade so as to realize its sustainability.

The Indian rupee also lost some value against the US dollar following the decline in Yuan, thereby a modest short-term impact on India. The devaluation of the Yuan may not have a much impact on Chinese exports, as the currency is still highly overvalued. However, if this adjustment of the currency continues then as per the J-curve effect, (J-Curve refers to the trend of a country's trade balance following a devaluation of currency under certain set of assumptions) Chinese exports will only increase as they become more competitive. This, in turn, will have a negative impact on Indian exports. Further, there will be an influx of Chinese goods into India, which will result in widening the already rising trade deficit with China.

India's major export items to China consist of primary commodities with cotton, copper and mineral fuels alone constituting more than 45 per cent of the total exports.

Meanwhile, India's major imports from China are electrical machinery and nuclear appliances (45 per cent of total imports). A reduction in the cost of Chinese goods can also accelerate the problem of dumping into India from China. Tyre makers, steel industry and organic chemicals, petro-chemicals industry are already reeling under the increasing dumping cases from China as lower currency incentivizes the country's exports.

The impact of this devaluation in the short term can be negative in some sectors like tyres, pharmaceuticals, textile and capital goods due to a sudden change in terms of trade and fear of dumping. However, in the long run there will not be material impact particularly in services till such time China dismantles the state monopoly over services. However, India has all options at its disposal under the WTO frame-work to tide over the short run impact. If the Yuan continues to lose value, then it might create pressure for the Reserve Bank of India governor to intervene to provide relief for the exporters and cut the key interest rate else the Indian goods would become less competitive.

The People's Bank of China cut its daily reference rate for the currency by a record 1.9 per cent, the biggest loss since January 1994. Many economists feared that China would take such a drastic step after the country announced its latest export numbers that, exports fell by 8.3 per cent in dollar terms in July 2015 on a y-o-y basis, sharply lower than Bloomberg's expectation of 1.5 per cent. Furthermore, China's central bank officials said that it plans to keep the Yuan stable at a "reasonable" level and will strengthen the market's role in determining the currency rate. This indicates that China is now looking at market forces to decide the direction of its currency rather than pegging it directly to the dollar. The 1.9 per cent fall could thus be one of the many we can expect in future.

Global markets are getting jittery over this move by China and expect a flight of capital adding to the slide in the Chinese equity market. Though China has a huge $ 3.69 trillion foreign exchange reserves that provides comfort, its recent round of selling US bonds has led the market to believe that they are in some kind of trouble, especially after the equity market sell-off in China. The message is clear from the action by Chinese authorities that they would like to support their economy under any condition. It also highlights that the Chinese economy is not as strong as the market believes.

SECTORS AFFECTED

Pharmaceuticals: This industry has been severely affected with a steadily declining exports to the Indian Ocean Region countries. (see Aid Policy Denting India's Exports)

Textiles: The biggest sector in which India competes with China head-on is textiles. Though China is moving on to high-end textiles, there is still a legacy segment where Indian companies can face competition on account of devaluation. Since margins are the smallest in the lower end of the textile segment, a devaluation of 1.9 per cent will eat into profits of some textile companies in India.

Chemicals: Chemicals, both organic and inorganic are largely produced in India and China. While margins in complex chemicals are higher, base chemicals attract lower margins. Low crude oil prices have already affected final prices, but China lowering its prices will impact Indian players.

Metals: Indian and global metal producers are impacted by a surge in Chinese exports. China is already facing a number of legal cases for selling its products at lower than cost price in many countries. Indian steel players have faced the brunt of the attack from Chinese imports. The recent hike in import duty has been nullified by the Yuan's depreciation.

Consumables: Most of the electrical consumables in India are imported from China. These can get cheaper in the coming days. But Indian companies generally do not pass on the benefit but pocket the difference. Companies who are importing their components or the entire equipment are clear gainers from China's move.

E-commerce: Mobiles, laptops, garments, toys and most of the goods that are sold by e-commerce companies are largely imported from China. They are the ones who will not be complaining about the fall in Chinese currency. One can expect some more mega-sale promotions being announced by e-commerce players in the days to come.

MARITIME SILK ROAD—CHINA'S NEW INITIATIVE

Chinese President Xi Jinping revived and accelerated the Maritime Silk Road (MSR) project primarily to boost the countries manufacturing sector and to improve trade relations with Southeast Asian neighbours Xi mooted these mega project during his visit to Kazakhstan in 2013. Since then several countries in the Eurasian Belt evinced interest in them. However, India has so far not made up its mind and cited lack of clarity as the reason for hesitation. China has proposed to finance many projects under the Silk Road Scheme in interested countries like Pakistan, Sri Lanka and others.

Xi Jinping launched with fanfare an ambitious New Silk Road Project on land and sea. Later termed it as One Belt One Road (OBOR), the massive strategic infrastructure project which aims to connect 60 countries spanning four continents. The MSR embeds for the search and development of new markets and investment destinations following the economic downturn in the West, which has so far, galvanized China's spectacular export led growth in the name of reviving civilizational linkages through extensive people-to-people contacts. The Silk Road, a romantic name, which is a Chinese strategic initiative comprising an infrastructure bank, consisting slew of roads, high speed rail, pipelines, ports, fiber-optic cables, industries, green parks, and smart cities throughout the route and corridors under Maritime Silk Road/Belt. China has also expected to link the Indian 'Spice Route' and 'Mausam' projects as a part of China-India Co-operation with MSR of China initiative.

China used to supply various kinds of goods to central Asian traders, as well as Arabs, Persians, Indians and Malays, who played a core role in the old Silk Road. In the New Silk Road (OBOR) of Xi Jinping's imagination, China will not only sell its dramatically produced products, but will also create pathways to move goods even to manufacture them in the partner countries, instead of the world coming to China as in the past, China will now be going out to the world. The MSR is an integral part of China's ambition to forge economic integrates on of Eurasia under its auspices and it is China's long-term goal of emerging as a global rival to the US. To attain the fundamental objective of the MSR or the OBOR, China has been undertaking several major infrastructural projects under it which requires huge investments such as: (i) 3000 km China Pakistan Economic Corridor from Kashgar to Gwadhar port in Pakistan which is going through Pakistan Occupied Kashmir (POK)—a 46 bn USD project funded by China. (ii) 2800 km Rail/Road Project from Kunming (China) to Kolkata (India) via Myanmar, Bangladesh called BCIM corridor. (iii) 1215 km Rail/Road corridor project from Yunnan (China) to the port of Kyaukpyu (Myanmar). (iv) 741 km Rail corridor from Lhasa (Tibet) to Kathmandu (Nepal) and to Patna (Bihar–India). (v) A 5000 km Naning (China) to Singapore Economic Corridor.

The Naning-Singapore Economic Corridor is an initiative of China, perceived in 2010, would connect several cities in Southern China with Nanning in China, Hanoi and Ho Chi Minh in Vietnam, Vietnam in Laos, Phnom Penh in

Cambodia, Bangkok in Thailand, Kuala Lumpur in Malaysia and Singapore, with modern road, rail, pipelines as well as cross-borders connectivity. The corridor is planned to better connect China with ASEAN economics and encourage development across the whole region with an aim to revamp its economy to a more developed 'New Normal' plain and an enroute to the emergence of an ASEAN-China Free Trade Area in the near future.

Chinese President Xi Jinping's ambition is to tie Central Asia and Europe with the Silk Road Economic Belt and to expand its trade and strategic reach in the South China Sea and Indian Ocean all the way to East Africa with the help of MSR. China has also created a $ 40 billion Silk Road Fund, which will finance construction of rail roads, pipelines and roadways that will link China with the three continents over land and sea.

China has also proposed to construct a canal across the Isthmus of Karin, Thailand which could provide faster link between South China Sea and Indian Ocean. A state-owned Chinese company is building a deep-water container port and industrial park in Malaysia. China has already taken over from India a $ 500 million airport development in Maldives, considered as an integral part of MSR. The Chinese President Xi Jinping, recently inaugurated one of the most ambitious project of China's costing $ 1.4 bn in Colombo Port City.

The "One Belt One Road" addresses a far reaching economic development plan and focuses on improving trade, infrastructure and connectivity in this region. The new Silk Road Economic Belt will link with Europe through Central and Western Asia and the so-called 21st Century Maritime Silk Road aims to connect China with South East Asian countries, Africa and Europe. The real purpose of this initiative, however, is security. China is using this plan as an attempt to improve relationship with its Asian neighbours. Its neighbours in East and South East Asia meanwhile hope this initiative will help mend relationships after much divisiveness over the South China Sea. China is also looking to increase friendly dealings with countries in Central Asia and West Asia, reason being it simply wants greater access to resources, specifically oil and gas. Beijing hopes this initiative will help in dealing with their security challenges by gaining better support and collaboration from the governments of the Central and Western Asian countries.

The Asian Infrastructure Investment Bank (AIIB) is an international financial institution—another China initiative that aims to support infrastructure in the Asia-Pacific region. The bank was initiated by the Chinese government, supported by 37 regional and 20 non-regional Perspective Funding Member (PFM) who signed, the 'article of agreement'. The Chinese government initiated the AIIB in view of the slow pace of reforms and governance in the established institutions like IMF, World Bank, and Asian Development Bank, which China claims that these institutions are dominated by the Western countries—serving America, European and Japanese interests. The AIIB is expected to solve the problems in supporting the projects undertaken under MSR by the Chinese government.

In the first of half this year 2015, China began implementing the ambitious Silk Road initiative, and the trade volumes with countries along the route has touched $ 485.4 billion, accounting for 25.8% of the country's total volume of foreign trade. During this period. China's exports volume to the countries along the 'Belt and Road' was $ 295.8 billion, accounting for 27.6% of its total exports. The imports value from these countries was $ 189bn, accounting for 23.4% of its imports.[11]

CONCLUSION

From the above discussions one clearly understands that, China's new initiatives and polices that were undertaken recently whether OROB under Maritime Silk Road or Aid Polices to third world countries, or even for that matter of devaluation of its currency trice in a short span of time is aimed to improve and to expand trade business with South Asia, Southeast Asia, Africa, West Asia and Central Asian countries, in the light of declining China's exports with Western countries due to the crisis of Eurozone currency. Secondly, to improve its exports volume with these regions, China has repeatedly devalued its currency in order to dump its products and to sell its excesses capacity in the manufacturing sector through the several corridors under OBOR programme, in order to maintain its falling growth rate—called as 'New Normal' level, as was evident from the Silk Road initiative which got $ 106 billion volume surplus in first half of 2015 itself.

China has had in its mind in undertaking several new initiatives to dominate the Indian Ocean and South China Sea in order to extract the resources available in the Oceans. Therefore, China has been extending and implementing Aid Polices to several developing countries those fall under various continents and even to the Pacific Ocean Island countries, with a long-term perspective to create a new international environment that is more favourable to China. Beijing is trying to promote these new initiatives as pure economic and trade initiatives but in reality it is trying to work for China's greater security and long term strategic objectives. To say the least, these Chinese initiatives of corridors under its ambitions programme of MSR may lead to security problems for India, as the corridors are engulfing India and Indian Ocean. Therefore, India should be careful of these recent initiatives which are aimed to slowly benefit China not only with respect to achieve and to maintain its falling growth rate and to tap the energy resources in the Indian Ocean Region countries.

REFERENCES

[1] Wang, Zhang, 2015, China's Alternative Diplomacy, www.the diplomate.com/2015/01/china'salternativediplomacy

[2] www.focus-economics.com/countries/china

[3] https://en.wikipedia.org/wiki/economy_of china

[4] www.wri.org/blog/2015/01/China's-overseas-investments-explai ned-10-graphics.

[5] Wolf Jr, Charles, Wang, Xiao, Warner, Erict, 'China's Foreign Aid and Government Sponsored Investment Activities,' www.diplomacy/RG pubs/Research-reports/RP118.HTML.

[6] www.lowyuistitute.org/issues/china-pacific

[7] Sinha, Varun, Currency War: How Yuan's Devaluation will impact India, www.profitndtv.com/news/economy/articlecurrency-war-how-yuan-devaluation-will-impact-indian-economy-1206553

[8] The Hindu, dated 9.1.2016.

[9] Ibid.

[10] www.qz.com/480615/india-and-thedevaluation-yuan-the-good-bad-and-the-ugly.

[11] http//economictimes.indiatimes.com/international.

Chinese New Maritime Silk Road Initiative: Opportunity or Threat to India?

M. Mayilvaganan

INTRODUCTION

The Geo-strategic and geopolitical focus of the global power has shifted from the west to the east. India and the People's Republic of China (PRC) are the two rising Asian powers who are constantly evolving their foreign policies to meet their burgeoning demands. China has shown remarkable growth since the end of the Cold War and has an upper hand compare to other Asian and European powers. The trajectory of its development is notable. The PRC claims this development or rise to be peaceful whereas its aggressive posture in the neighbourhood issues has resulted in a hostile environment in the surroundings. All these factors have created complex circumstances for countries in the Asia-Pacific region.

Also, the rise of China has altered the ecosystem in the Asia and today Beijing evolved as an opposition force to the dominance of the US in the world affairs. Yet, at the same time it has provided arenas for cooperation and collaboration through large scale Chinese investments in countries of Southeast Asia, South Asia and Oceania. Indeed, Beijing has spread its wings as far as Africa, where it is involved in constructing roads, railways, and public buildings.

The 'Pivot to Asia', as part of the 'Grand Strategy' of the USA to refine its strategic dynamics and engagement with Asia along with the Trans-Pacific Partnership (TPP) have prompted China to come out with the revival of Silk Road diplomacy. China has sought to increase its sphere of influence and to enhance co-operation with the Asia-Pacific, Central Asia, and the Indian Ocean Region (IOR) by this initiative. More importantly, through this proposal Beijing is eyeing on establishing and securing its trade along the Indian Ocean littorals through more organised manner.

The MSR a part of its One Belt One Road initiative was mooted by President Xi Jinping during his visit to Indonesia and Malaysia in 2013 where he stated that the MSR would help turn the "Golden Decade" between China and the countries in the region into "Diamond Decade". Consequently, Beijing has invited all countries in Southeast Asia, South Asia, West Asia and Europe to join its MSR scheme. According to the Chinese, basically the MSR aims to improve connectivity, trade among Asian nations through the sea on the lines of the ancient Silk Route. Reported some have responded positively, whereas countries like India have not officially said yes to the Chinese proposal. However, the pertinent questions are: How China is going to implement this project when it has mistrust with many of the countries in the region including India? And who—the agency—within China is going to execute them? How it is going to do so and what the benefits actually the countries who are going to be part of the scheme will receive.

China's new Silk Route initiative—the Silk Route Economic Belt (SREB) and Maritime Silk Road (MSR)—have attracted much of the international attention. The MSR has the historical importance of the Indian Ocean to China. This is a part of its wider attempt by China to construct multiple lines of communication to develop inner Chinese provinces and shape China's regional periphery by exercising economic, political and cultural influence. This study is an attempt to analyze in detail the course of MSR, its political, economic and strategic implications for China and the rest of the world.

The China's new Silk Road diplomacy consists of a network of land and maritime routes stretching from Europe to Asia's eastern coast. In particular, China desires to connect to the west through the historical route by amplifying its associations to bring about stability in the borders, to reduce the development gap between eastern and western China, to secure its trade and energy resources, and to improve inland transport system.

IMPORTANCE OF IOR FOR CHINA

There is a prominent rise of geo-political interest and commercial investments of the states around the Indian Ocean and role of extra-regional powers such as China, USA, Japan, and EU, etc. The IOR today has become centre stage in the global politics. According to Heidelberg Institute for International Conflict Research, more than 50 per cent of the world conflicts occur in the Indian Ocean.[1] Notable conflicts are—competing rises of India and China, nuclear confrontation between India and Pakistan, Israel and Palestine, US intervention in Iraq and Afghanistan, piracy problems in Somalia and around the Horn of Africa, Islamic terrorism and many more.

The substantial increase in the significance of The Indian Ocean owes to the presence of much of the world's important Sea Lines of Communications (SLOC), major Choke Points, oil deposits in the Gulf and the capability of the immediate states to shape the petroleum exports. Petroleum exports from The Indian Ocean to Asia through Red Sea and Suez Canal, around the Horn of Africa is the most vulnerable region prone to conflicts-political, military, terrorist and piracy. For quite a long time, the US largely dominated the IOR without any substantial competitor.

The rise of strong aggressive China in the region has challenged the US power and brought the Indian Ocean back to the centre stage of geo-strategic and geo-political importance. With the sudden increase in demand for energy products, sea (ocean) became important for countries consequently, it led to major powers effort to secure the transit lines which traverses through IOR. Thus, a quest for supremacy has led to the presence of naval bases of various states greater than before.

The IOR is witnessing naval arms race. The J-20 project, DF-21D—said to be the world's first anti-ship ballistic missile— and Shang-class nuclear-powered attack submarines of China and India's Shang-class nuclear-powered attack submarines project are case in point. Apparently, China has seven nuclear and 51 conventional submarines which are divided into three fleets. These have the capacity to perform long range under-water operations.[2] Maritime security in the Indian Ocean is therefore characterised by militarization within the region, a considerable involvement and presence of extra-regional powers. Exercising good order at sea poses a paramount challenge to the existing maritime security forces. In fact, many coastal navies focus on policing roles and the security of littorals.

As a dominant power the US has benefit of access to several ports and basing agreements with many littoral states. Besides, the US Navy is the significant player in projecting power dynamics in the Indian Ocean. It performs regular joint naval exercises and shares intelligence information with its alliance partners. In a way, the US is seen as a strategic anchor of the region although some are doubtful of its hegemonic interests.

Interestingly, China is using its aggressive soft power diplomacy to bolster its influence to secure the oil trade and safeguard the transport. By sanctioning large loans with less interest rate and promising assistance in infrastructure development, China is following fairly a grand strategy in wooing the littorals with its economic power. It has been helping and assisting its allies to improve their capacities in the region. Myanmar and Sri Lanka are some of the classic examples where China provided substantial assistance as part of its grand strategy, since for China, the Indian Ocean is the key to its interests-international and domestic.

MSR AND MARITIME STRATEGIES

China has been carefully crafting its future military and maritime strategies for more than a decade. It is successful in expanding its wide-ranging influence in the Southeast Asia, South Asia and Africa by means of loans for national development, military exercises, political and technological assistance. China has also noticeably increased its submarine presence in the IOR in what the Indian media has dubbed a 'submarine noose'.[3] China is insuring its future energy security by being in a position to deploy its naval units next to Choke Points where its interests may be threatened. So, it has been improving the capacities of its own allies in the region in an effort to check any impact of India's fleet expansion would have on Chinese operations.

China's MSR seems to be a part of its overall maritime strategy to consolidate its influence and at the same time to neutralise the dominance of the US in the IOR. Even before the MSR initiative, the Chinese have addressed their energy interests through investments along the Indian Ocean littorals. Through, theses investment and projects in littoral states like Pakistan, Myanmar, Sri Lanka, Bangladesh and Maldives, etc. Beijing was able to acquire positive response to their MSR project. Gwadar port in Pakistan, Hambantota port and Colombo port city project in Sri Lanka, and other developmental projects in the region are a part of its grand strategy. China has been working hard to deal with other countries to acquire their consent and participation in their ambitious project.

CHINA'S MARITIME SILK ROAD (MSR) PROJECT

Chinese President Xi Jinping's during his trip to Southeast Asia in October 2013 proposed this concept of linking several countries in line with its ancient silk route.[4] As per the proposal the MSR is expected to stretch from Asia's eastern coast to Europe, connecting Pacific to the Baltic Sea. Begins in Quanzhou in Fujian province, then hitting Guangzhou (Guangdong province), Beihai (Guangxi), and Haikou (Hainan) before heading south to the Malacca Strait, afterwards from Kuala Lumpur, it heads to probably Kolkata/Kozhikode in India, then crosses the rest of the Indian Ocean to Nairobi in Kenya. From Nairobi, again the MSR travels north around the Horn of Africa and moves through the Red Sea into the Mediterranean, with a halt in Athens before meeting the land-based Silk Road in Venice. It is estimated to cover 4.4 billion people and US $ 2.1 trillion gross production which accounts for 63 percent of world population and 29 percent of world GDP.[5]

For the project, Beijing has pledged US $ 40 billion in the Silk Road Fund to develop infrastructure along the route apart from being backed by more than $ 100 billion fund drawn from China's Asia Infrastructure Investment Bank (AIIB),[6] through which China has created a situation where countries are increasingly seeing it as an 'irresistible opportunity' for development.

In China's view, the MSR is expected to increase maritime connectivity and cooperation on issues like disaster mitigation and the development of fisheries between the Indo-Pacific, East Africa and the Mediterranean. Building infrastructure, upgrading port facilities and creating economic compatibility with countries along the maritime zone are said to be the other objectives of this Chinese proposal. According to the Chinese foreign ministry spokesperson Hua Chunying, the MSR initiative is "just an idea for cooperation. It is an open ended platform. The purpose is to integrate all kinds of ongoing cooperation especially cooperation on connectivity in the spirit of (ancient) silk road so that they can connect with each other and promote each other and accelerate regional countries' common development."[7] Evidently it is China's ambition to reclaim its place as the hub—Middle Kingdom— linked to the world by trade and cultural exchanges.

The essential rationale of Beijing's MSR initiative is to leverage their soft-power. In a sense, the apparently aim is "to shore-up China's image as a benevolent state"[8] and possibly utilize its commercial investments part of the project to establish its legitimate interests in the Indian Ocean region. After decades of high growth driven by massive investments and excess productions China still faces many domestic challenges like unbalanced development and pollution. Inevitably it needs other channels to achieve its objectives. Through this initiative China intends to develop its land-locked western provinces and enable them to access the markets of Southeast Asia, the Middle East, and Eastern Europe, thus "shaping China's regional periphery by exercising economic, cultural and political influence."[9] As what was stated in the Third Plenum of the 18th CPC Central Committee in November 2013 that China will strive to expand and accelerate the opening of the inland and border regions so as to build an economic corridor criss-crossing the country.

Equally, it is also perceived as a Chinese attempt to 'reorder' Asia—to bolster its influence and authority in the region— and undermine US influence in the region. Particularly, the US 'pivot' to Asia—which focuses on concentrating additional forces and equipment in the Asia Pacific—and establishing the Trans-Pacific Partnership (TPP), which aims to contain China's effort to "write the rules of the global economy."[10] China aims to have a more equal footing vis-à-vis US in international economy through this concept.

The MSR is a strategic concept designed in a way to shape the geo-strategic position of China in the world & the Asia-Pacific region in particular. It is also identified as China's own Marshall Planwhich tries to advance its neighbourhood diplomacy and aims to raise maritime partnership with littorals in the IOR to a new level. Thus through more trade and investment, Beijing hopes to build long term partnership with littoral states. By deepening its sphere of influence, firstly, it can secure the flow of resources and strategic materials through protected shipping and SLOC's and secondly, it provides security and logistic support to its overseas assets, as the secured trade route is expected to be free of any potential US blockade.

Furthermore, greater connectivity between China and the other littoral states in the region is expected to help the establishment and improvement of Asia's supply chain, industrial chain and value chain, thus bringing Pan-Asian and Eurasian regional cooperation to a new level, and benefiting China in the process. It also provides a channel of overseas investment for Chinese companies.

INTERNATIONAL RESPONSE TO BEIJING'S MSR INITIATIVE

The interests and responses showed by China's neighbours and others are varied. Some view that China's expanding forays is necessary for the world economy and to rebalance the geo-political power with the west. They say it as an inevitable consequence as the super growth of China has run its course. Whereas some others opine that China too is following the footsteps of US whereby becoming hegemony, which is evident from its behaviour in the Asia-Pacific region. Both ways, MSR is substantial for regional stability and global peace.

In particular, Southeast Asian states are excited about the economic opportunities brought in by China, but at the same time, are wary about the growing geo-political implications of Chinese influence in the region. ASEAN countries desperately need infrastructure development but Chinese behaviour in the neighbourhood has forced them to take a step backwards. But China continues to reassure about its intention and the benefits to them. ASEAN wants China to modify its aggressive approach and even they proposed a 'code of conduct' in South China Sea to China in March 2014 to attain a "gradual progress and reach consensus through consultations."[11] In short, there is an increasing anxiety among ASEAN countries over the Chinese proposal. While China has occupied much of the economic space with Southeast Asia by becoming number one trading partner and investor but the US still continues the security guarantee for them. Because of this fear many evolved a dual strategy of depending on China for economic development and on US for security.[12]

Pakistan, Bangladesh, Sri Lanka and Maldives in South Asia are fervent about the vast foreign investments brought by the Chinese MSR, even though domestic resistance also persists. A section of locals are concerned about China's pursuit of its own interests which may harm their own search for opportunities to fulfil their interests.[13] India on the other hand has largely been sceptic of the increase in Chinese influence in the region and Chinese proposal of MSR. By and large, the responses from South Asia towards this can be understood from the following points: first, China is gradually becoming stronger geo-strategically with noticeable increase in its influence in the regional politics; and second, China-smaller South Asian countries relations are intensifying providing opportunities for both to explore common interests and welfare. In short, the countries in South Asia have given a mixed response to the Chinese proposal.

INDIA AND CHINA'S MSR

Increasingly, India and China (also other countries like Japan and Australia) have entered into a new phase of shadow power politics in the IOR driven by their respective economic and strategic interest. In the process each seems to be employing new tactics, and extending their reach in the regions and beyond. Interestingly, the two countries are engaged in co-operation in certain areas yet competitive power in maritime sphere as increasingly seas—IOR—are becoming 'vital for their own energy security and economic sustainability.'[14] Each one desires for an absolute authority of their neigh-bourhood in the region.

In this context, China's MSR initiative is evidently part of Beijing's plan of rationalizing its overseas projects in the Indian Ocean region and securing its assets. In addition, the MSR is intended to provide space for Chinese domestic companies who were hit with uncertainty in countries like Myanmar, Sri Lanka, etc. with the change of regime to far off territory/market in Europe. Even though Chinese initiative seems to be an attempt to counter the mighty US, and not India, New Delhi has been reluctant to bandwagon with China currently.

China has invited India to join its newly propounded MSR, first with the invitation issued during the Special-Repre-sentative-level talks between the two sides in Beijing and later a formal invitation during the 17th round of talks between special representatives in New Delhi in February 2014. Even though many countries in the region responded positively to the Beijing's call, India kept silent probably due to lack of clarity about the Chinese strategy and who is intend to do what. According to India's External Affairs Minister, Sushma Swaraj, there is no need to give "a blanket endorsement" to the Chinese plan[15] and India's official position was that it was awaiting further details from China on the plan. India's silence has mainly been due to uncertainty about how the MSR will be implemented, along with concerns as to whether it will have a geo-economic rationale or a security orientation.

Economically or commercially, India is located at a prime position in the IOR and is expected to benefit from the Chinese MSR. Apparently, MSR is going to traverse India's periphery. Firstly, it offers a number of opportunities for India, particularly developing coastal states in infrastructural development and connectivity, creating employment and industries, etc. When India has already indicated its wish to draw Chinese investments, being part of the MSR will certainly help in this regard. Secondly, it would help India to develop its northeast part and further aid in its Act East Policy. Thirdly, it could prove to be a perfect platform to enhance India's regional and bilateral cooperation along with China. Fourthly, by being an active partner to the initiative, India too can invest in neighbouring littoral countries thereby boosting its sphere of influence. But the question is whether China wants India to be an equal partner in the project or just it wants to investment in India as part of the MSR. Thus, from the economic perspective, it would be best for India to accept the invitation and join the MSR.

However, from the strategic and security perspective the MSR seems to be a hindrance to India is interest. Importantly, though the MSR is about the development of maritime infrastructure and connectivity in the Indian Ocean and the Western Pacific, but it looks like part of its maritime military strategy. The larger questions are how much India stands to gain from this project and whether New Delhi is ready to work with Beijing? Already when China is posing a strategic challenge to India and its influence in the region apart from distrustful of each other's intentions including maritime manoeuvre and enduring border problem between the two, it is difficult for India to think of joining the MSR. Also with the history of Chinese projects in the neighbourhood where Beijing brings in its own men and material including equipment's, providing access to them through the MSR looks to be perilous.

In addition, the 'opaque' nature of its proposal, essentially is the problem with the MSR where India finds it difficult to take a call. In spite of its pronouncement in 2013, China still has not released the complete details of the project, and this makes many countries including India doubtful of Beijing's strategic intentions. The lack of specifics about the MSR not only makes it hard to decipher its real purpose, but it also gives credence to suspicions of geopolitical game played by China. MSR could be a surrogate of Chinese strategy of controlling SLOC that run all the way from the East African coast, to the Southern coast of China and a means to set up Chinese logistical hubs in the Indian Ocean, linking up already existing projects.

In short, there is an opportunity for greater collaboration with China bilaterally and also in establishing a multi-polar world but it could well turn out to be detrimental to India's geopolitical interests in the IOR. In absence of not being an equal partner, the MSR project may adversely affect India's strategic purchase in its area of influence. And the question is whether it is more beneficial for India to align with the Chinese MSR or with Japan's Bay of Bengal Industrial Growth Belt (BIG B) initiative, when it has an alternative today. Compared to China, India's interactions and co-operation with Japan and Australia in the IOR or maritime domain is high. Maybe the amicable settlement of border issues could provide much more confidence and rationale for India to respond promptly and positively to the Chinese proposal in future.

CONCLUSION

Today the Indian Ocean's traditional status as an international trade highway is more significant than ever before. The military presence in the ocean is unprecedented. As a result, despite the region's marked development and economic growth, security concerns dominate the agendas of its states. China continues to be the key security concern for many. Chinese aggressive posture and its involvement in regional affairs are case in point.

After establishing AIIB and BRICS Bank, China now has considerable say in the economic affairs of the world. Its Silk Road initiative is perceived as China's own 'Marshal Plan' as a result, in spite of gained momentum, MSR has still not received the consent of countries like India who have a major say in the region. MSR is the test of Chinese neighbourhood policy. If Beijing is successful in its attempt to secure almost all their consent and implement its initiative, it indeed will hold the course of future international policies in its hands and emerge as a true challenger to the US. If not, China continues to remain as an aggressor in the view of neighbours and may lose credibility of not being able to craft its own multilateral initiative. All depends on how far Beijing will go to accomplish its Silk Route diplomacy and more importantly in securing India's endorsement. It remains to be seen how India is going to take action on MSR and how much benefit the project is going to bring into the associates.

REFERENCES

[1] *Conflict Barometer 2014*, Heidelberg Institute for International Conflict Research at http://www.hiik.de/en/

[2] Westcott, Stephen, "Australia-India-China: IOR Procurement Race for Submarines," *IPCS*, 24 March 2015 at www.ipcs.org/print_articledetails.php?recNo=4881

[3] Unnithan, Sandeep, "China's submarine noose around India," *India Today*, December 4, 2014 at http://indiatoday.intoday.in/

story/china-submarine-noose-using-undersea-vessels-to-project-power-in-india/1/405191.html

[4] According to China the MSR symbolizes the continuity of their maritime traditions, which were amplified by the voyages to the Asia-Pacific, South Asia, West Asia and East Africa by the famous 15th-century Chinese mariner, Zheng He.

[5] Cheng, Shuaihua Wallace, "China's New Silk Road: Implications for the US," *Yale Global,* 28 May 2015 at http://yaleglobal.yale.edu/content/china%E2%80%99s-new-silk-road-implications-us

[6] The AIIB provides for only three seats for non-regional countries in the board contrary to the existing situation in the multilateral financial institution with 75 percent seats reserved for Asian countries. There were some fears of China's motive to use AIIB to promote its power in Asia.

[7] Refer PTI, "China invites India to join its Maritime Silk Road initiative," *Live Mint,* February 14 2014 at http://www.livemint.com/Politics/V9WAuunYW07IzGOktIFDHK/China-invites-India-to-join-its-Maritime-Silk-Road-initiativ.html

[8] Singh, Abhijit, "China's Maritime Silk Route: Implications for India," *IDSA Comment,* July 16, 2014 at http://www.idsa.in/idsacomments/ChinasMaritimeSilkRoute_AbhijitSingh_160714

[9] Nataraj, Geethanjali, "India should get on board China's Maritime Silk Road," *East Asia Forum,* 27 June 2015 at http://www.eastasiaforum.org/2015/06/27/india-should-get-on-board-chinas-maritime-silk-road

[10] Hsu, Sara, "China and the Trans-Pacific Partnership," *The Diplomat,* October 14, 2015 at http://thediplomat.com/2015/10/china-and-the-trans-pacific-partnership

[11] Tiezzi, Shannon, "Why China Isn't Interested in a South China Sea Code of Conduct", *The Diplomat,* February 26, 2014 at http://thediplomat.com/2014/02/why-china-isnt-interested-in-a-south-china-sea-code-of-conduct

[12] Li, Xue and Yanzhou, Xu, "How China Can Perfect Its 'Silk Road' Strategy", *The Diplomat,* April 9, 2015 at http://thediplomat.com/2015/04/how-china-can-perfect-its-silk-road-strategy

[13] Also other concern that dwells in the minds of people includes the resultants of large scale projects of China—disruption to their environmental stability by altering the traditional culture and way of life.

[14] Panda, Jagannath, "Maritime Silk Road and the India-China Conundrum," *Indian Foreign Affairs Journal,* Vol. 9, No. 1, January-March 2014, p. 23.

[15] Refer Ananth Krishnan, "China asks India to put aside 'Maritime Silk Road' concerns," *India Today,* February 12, 2015 at http://indiatoday.intoday.in/story/china-india-asean-sushma-swaraj-maritime-silk-road-concerns/1/418576.html

India's Expanding Role and Influence in Asia-Pacific

Sylvia Mishra

China's growing naval profile in the Indian Ocean and assertiveness in maritime territorial disputes in East and South China Sea has once again reinforced the discourse of an enhanced Indian role in the Asia-Pacific. The region is witnessing a strategic flux as both the Asian giants, India and China, are setting their footprints in each other's traditional domain of interest namely, the Indian Ocean and Asia-Pacific Region respectively. These developments come at a time when the United States is rebalancing toward the Asia; Japan under Prime Minister Abe is modifying its post-war pacifist constitution; and most of Southeast Asian countries are increasingly looking towards India to become a credible counter-weight to balance China. As several Asia-Pacific countries have casted doubts on China's so-called 'peaceful rise', there is an overgrowing dependence on the security umbrella provided by the United States. This delicate security fabric in the region is further exacerbated by the lack of existing security architecture.

India's Foreign Secretary Dr. S. Jaishankar in a public address claimed that India is transitioning from being a 'balancing power to a leading power'.[1] Commensurate with India's desire, it is imperative that India undertakes more responsebilities in the region. India's more active economic and political role in the region has been repeatedly encouraged and welcomed by countries like the United States, Japan and other

Southeast Asian countries. Despite steps undertaken by successive Indian governments to direct its foreign, economic and military strategies eastward, India has been unable to deeply integrate itself in the Asia-Pacific like the United States or China. So far India's role in the region has been limited—reactive and at best episodic. However, India has the desire and the potential to become an important actor and thereby help shape the future security architecture in the Asia-Pacific region.

The existing scholarship is vastly divided on the role of the South Asian giant in the Asia-Pacific. While some narratives on the issue have been quick to dismiss India as a significant Asia-Pacific power (Derek McDougall; Asia-Pacific in World Politics; 2007), more nuanced treatment on the subject has come from scholars like David Brewster. In his book, *India as an Asia-Pacific Power* (2013), Brewster traces India's interactions with a region which has traditionally not included India and concludes India's rise as an Asia-Pacific power to be an open-ended question. These views on the subject are starkly different from scholars like Harsh Pant as he contend that India is already "*a major player in the Asia-Pacific regional balance of power along with the US, China and Japan.*"[2] Bridging the gap between the two extremes—dismissing India's emerging role in Asia-Pacific and ascribing India as already an established Asia-Pacific actor—analyst Walter C. Ladwig III has suggested that the '*truth lies somewhere between these two extremes.*'[3] Some Indian authors of *Nonalignment 2.0* argue India cannot become a great power if it is unable to manage relationships within South Asia while others believe that India, too like the United States, Great Britain, and Germany can rise despite being in an unsettled neighbor-hood.[4]

In spite of the varying degree of merit in both the school of narratives, the locus of the debate centers on India's capability to recalibrate its economic, political and military power in the Asia-Pacific. It is also hinged on India's willingness to project power farther than its shores. Traditionally India has been diffident to project power in the Asia-Pacific and has exercised restraint for the apprehension of antagonizing China. However, the inexorable rise of China's military power and increasing Chinese influence across India's own periphery has deeply influenced India's proactive eastward orientation. China's rapid military modernization is raison d'être for India to actively seek a multipolar Asia-Pacific. India's ability to successfully embed itself as an Asia-Pacific power in the same ranks like the US, China and Japan would be determined by India's capacity to bolster India's Act East Policy, develop a Blue Water Navy, deepen partnership with the ASEAN countries and regional powers like Japan and Australia and recalibrate strategic closeness with the US. Acting through these levers, India's strategic designs can become strategically commensurate with its desire to undertake more responsibilities in the region. Furthermore, these goals are also in consonance with Washington's political goals in the region.

If shifting balance of power in the Asia-Pacific is shaping India's political goals in the Asia-Pacific, India too is shaping the region by developing its own comprehensive national power, active blue water navy diplomacy and collaborating with regional powers like Japan and Australia. As India figures prominently in the US geostrategic security calculus, global security interests of both the countries have found maximum convergence in the Asia-Pacific region. During President Obama's visit to India in January 2015 as the chief-guest for India's Republic Day celebration, the two leaders signed a landmark Joint Strategic Vision for the Asia-Pacific and Indian Ocean.[5] The vision document serves as an important roadmap in pursuit of collaborative security, economic and political goals which are of core interest to both countries.

India also features prominently in the US National Security Strategy 2015 document[6] and the Department of Defense publication The Asia-Pacific Maritime Security Strategy.[7] Due to the changing balance of power in the region, India's defence and security cooperation with the US is steadily growing. The United States is India's largest US defence supplier and both the countries are engaging in expanded military exercises and models of joint co-production and co-development of defence hardware.[8] During the first official visit of India's Defence Minister Manohar Parrikar to the Pentagon, US Defense Secretary Ashton Carter said "*The defense partnership between the United States and India will become an anchor of global security.*" These are signs that the region can expect India and the US to work jointly in the region to secure a stable Asia-Pacific without being dominated by China.[9]

India-US collaborative partnership in the Asia-Pacific region is aimed at accommodating China in a security order which is inclusive and rules-based. Both countries are also determined to retain status quo in the Asia-Pacific and hedge against a China which is increasingly unilateral and assertive in its actions. In spite of these overarching similarities in strategic interests in the region, Indian security planners have genuine concerns regarding the US-China relations. Several commentators have casted uncertainty of the future course of relations between Washington and Beijing fearing a G-2 which could lead to power-sharing in the region. As Chinese President Xi Jinping's statements record his vision of a model of major power relations to "*manage, control and handle disputes*" between the US and China, the concept of forming a condominium between the two countries have waxed and waned over time.[10]

Additionally to become an Asia-Pacific power, India has been gradually building its defense and security relationships with a number of Southeast Asian nations. Over the past decade, India has expanded its naval presence into the South China Sea and exercised with Southeast Asian navies, particularly Singapore, Malaysia, Indonesia, Thailand, Vietnam, and the Philippines.[11] However, both India and some of the ASEAN states believe that India should play a greater diplomatic and security role in the region. This includes a larger naval presence which involves building a "blue water navy", a force capable of operating in open seas and projecting power to areas of strategic interest. New Delhi targets a strong presence in the strategically located Malacca Straits which accounts for 40 percent of the world's trade and more than 80 percent of China's oil imports. An article in the Economist argues that India's naval advantage in the Malacca Straits—a strategic chokepoint—might allow New Delhi to impede oil traffic.[12] However, India's capacity to project military power far from its home waters is still at a nascent stage. A long time desire for a blue-water navy has met with a staggering progress as in the recent years, the Indian navy has seen a reduction in its allocated budget from 19 percent in 2012 to 2013 to 16 percent in 2015–2016. Additionally, the Indian navy is reported to have a shortage of 1,322 officers and 11,257 sailors along with the dismal condition of acute shortage of ships and helicopters.[13] These operational challenges have greatly stymied India's desire for a blue water-navy.

For Indian policymakers in the security arena, the challenge in building India as a key Asia-Pacific actor will boil down to four elements: willingness to project and sustain its military presence beyond the Indian Ocean; India's ability to put concerted focus on Asia-Pacific moving away from its immediate neighbourhood, especially its north-western neighbour with which India has remained long fixated; New Delhi's capability to break the gridlock of a defensive mindset of hedging against China and finally, India's resolve to deepen its economic cooperation with Southeast Asian countries. Southeast Asia is a major global hub for manufacturing and trade and account for a total trade of $ 2 trillion (2010), a six-fold increase over the region's 1990 global trade of $ 300 billion.[14]The economic advantages shared between Southeast Asian states and China has clear advantages over those with India. China-ASEAN total trade accounts for $ 480 billion[15] in 2014 while India stood at a paltry $ 80 billion.[16] As India's future lies in this region, New Delhi would need to take active steps to move beyond rhetoric of historical linkages and cultural ties. Instead focus on developmental progress which would be mutually symbiotic for both India and the ASEAN countries. Deeply integrating India into the Global Value Chains (GVCs) should be a priority for the Indian government since such participation has supplemented a robust growth in GDP for most Asia-Pacific countries in the past decade. India's participation in GVCs in terms of the share in total value added created by GVCs was 1.1% in 2013 while that of China was 8.9% (the highest in the world).[17] Through these efforts India could start expanding its economic footprints in the region while expanding its presence and influence.

India's security role in the Pacific in the long term would be critical in sustaining and maximizing its strategic interests in the Indian Ocean. As competition for strategic space continues to rise in the Indian Ocean, New Delhi must continue the momentum of building partnership with the US, Southeast Asian states and the regional powers. This will be instrumental in shaping the narrative of India's emergence as a credible security provider in the Pacific. Looking at the underlying Sino-Indian tensions in the Indian Ocean, India's important partnerships with resident Pacific players would only provide India with a strategic leverage of managing China's naval profile in the Indian Ocean.

REFERENCES

[1] 'IISS Fullerton Lecture by Dr. S. Jaishankar, Foreign Secretary in Singapore', *Ministry of External Affairs*, July 20, 2015, available at http://mea.gov.in/Speeches-Statements.htm?dtl/25493/IISS_Fullerton_Lecture_by_Foreign_Secretary_in_Singapore

[2] Pant, Harsh V., 'India in the Asia-Pacific: Rising Ambitions with an Eye on China'; *Asia-Pacific Review*, Vol. 14, Issue 1, pp. 54–71, July 13, 2007.

[3] Ladwig III, Walter C., 'Delhi's Pacific Ambition: Naval Power, "Look East," and India's Emerging Influence in Asia-Pacific', *Asian Security*, Vol. 5, No. 2, pp. 87–113, 2009.

[4] 'Nonalignment 2.0: A Foreign and Strategic Policy for India in the Twenty First Century' *Centre for Policy Research*, 2012.

[5] 'US-India Joint Strategic Vision for the Asia-Pacific and the Indian Ocean Region', *The White House*, January 25, 2015, available at https://www.whitehouse.gov/the-press-office/2015/01/25/us-india-joint-strategic-vision-asia-pacific-and-indian-ocean-region

[6] 'The National Security Strategy' *The White House*, February 2015, available https://www.whitehouse.gov/sites/default/files/docs/2015_national_security_strategy.pdf

[7] 'The Asia-Pacific Maritime Security Strategy', *Department of Defense*, available at http://www.defense.gov/Portals/1/Documents/pubs/NDAA%20A-P_Maritime_SecuritY_Strategy-081420 15-1300-FINALFORMAT.PDF

[8] Pandit, Rajat, 'US set to be India's biggest arms supplier', *Times of India*, July 13, 2015, available at http://timesofindia.indiatimes.com/india/US-set-to-be-Indias-biggest-arms-supplier/articleshow/48047176.cms

[9] Cronk, Terri Moon, 'Carter Calls US-India Defense Partnership Anchor of Global Security', *Department of Defense News*, December 10, 2015, available at http://www.defense.gov/News-Article-View/Article/633727/carter-calls-us-india-defense-partnership-anchor-of-global-security

[10] Yoon, Sangwon, 'Xi Tells Kerry China and US Can Both Be Pacific Power', *Bloomberg*, May 17, 2015, available at http://www.bloomberg.com/news/articles/2015-05-17/xi-sees-room-for-both-china-u-s-as-powers-in-pacific-region

[11] 'Look East, Cross Black Waters: India's Interest in Southeast Asia', *Rand Corporation*, available at http://www.rand.org/content/dam/rand/pubs/research_reports/RR1000/RR1021/RAND_RR1021.pdf

[12] 'Know Your Own Strength: India As A Great Power', *The Economist*, March 30, 2013, available at http://www.economist.com/news/briefing/21574458-india-poised-become-one-four-largest-military-powers-world-end

[13] 'Armed Forces Face Shortage of Over 52,000 Personnel' *Indian Express*, March 20, 2015, available at http://indianexpress.com/article/india/armed-forces-face-shortage-of-over-52000-personnel

[14] Mahbubani, Kishore and Severino, Rhoda, 'ASEAN: The Way Forward', *McKinsey Commentaries*, May 2014, available at http://www.mckinsey.com/industries/public-sector/our-insights/asean-the-way-forward

[15] 'China's Growing Ties With ASEAN Opens Up New Opportunities For Foreign Investment', *China Briefing*, August 7, 2015, available at http://www.china-briefing.com/news/2015/08/07/chinas-growing-ties-with-asean-opens-up-new-opportunities-for-foreign-investment.html

[16] Hunt, Luke, 'Indian Trade Seem Booming With ASEAN', *The Diplomat*, August 26, 2014, available at http://thediplomat.com/2014/08/indian-trade-seen-booming-with-asean

[17] 'Measuring Value in Global Value Chains', *Centre for WTO Studies*, Working Paper, May 2013, available at http://wtocentre.iift.ac.in/workingpaper/Measuring%20Value%20in%20Global%20Value%20Chains%20CWS%20WP%20Final.pdf

China's '21st Century Maritime Silk Road': Strategy for Security

Amrita Jash

ABSTRACT

In international politics, oceans have always acted as a key determinant of the survival and development of nation states-serving for economic wealth, commercial growth, and national security. Given this, maritime supremacy has become the new code of international politics. In this context, Chinese leadership have increasingly shifted their focus to the maritime domain, wherein, aspirations of becoming a "strong maritime power" has become a key national security goal. Driven by this objective, Chinese President Xi Jinping proposed the idea of '21st Century Maritime Silk Road' (MSR) initiative during his visit to Indonesia in October 2013. Wherein, China's maritime adventurism to connect Asia to Europe and Africa aims to build sea trade connectivity through ports and other infrastructure build up. But given the rising tensions in the critical waters of South China Sea, Indian Ocean, where China faces severe challenges, MSR as claimed to be an economic initiative becomes highly questionable.

What is noteworthy, is that with an unparalleled economic growth, China has increasingly become dependent on the seas for trade and energy supplies. For China, security of the Sea Lines of Communication (SLOCs) and having uninterrupted access to them has become a key objective for securing China's growth and development. In this regard, given China's maritime aspirations, the '21st Century Maritime Silk Road' initiative is a strategy to safeguard its own national security interests and strategic objectives. And most importantly, the Maritime Silk Road initiative helps China to realise the Chinese Dream of "great rejuvenation of the Chinese nation" and building a well-off society based on Chinese values. In this view, the present paper discusses the strategic and security objectives behind building of the '21ˢᵗ Century Maritime Silk Road', where the central argument is that China's maritime agenda is driven by geopolitical and geostrategic interests rather than just an economic rational.

INTRODUCTION

With the turn of the century, international politics has witnessed significant shifts in the global balance of power. Of which, one of the primary factors that influenced the systemic change is the 'rise of China'. With a double digit growth, China ascended to become an economic power house, ranking second in the order as world's largest economy after United States in 2010. China's booming economy invariably catalysed its military might. These state of affairs prompted speculations of 'China threat' against 'China's rise' mainly centered on concerns over China's military muscle flexing in the international maritime zone. That is, speculations over China's intentions as witnessed in its growing military assertiveness in the maritime domain. The anxiety over China's growing maritime interests were primarily argued over its intentions in the Indian Ocean, called the 'String of Pearls' strategy to build and expand China's naval and military installations across the Indian Ocean. Though this concept has been debated and declined by China but with the visible shifts in China's policy from being a continental power to that of becoming a sea power, it can be clearly stated that China has a real interest in building and securing its military presence in the crucial sea lanes of communications—a vital national interest to secure the growth and stability of China's economy.

Given this strategic objective to secure China's economic interest by securing China's military presence and activities in the crucial SLOCs, Chinese President Xi Jinping's grand vision of building the 'New Silk Road" under "One Belt, One Road Initiative"—which rightly add to the speculations over China's maritime intentions. The framework aims to run the Belt and Road through the continents of Asia, Europe and Africa, connecting the vibrant East Asia economic circle at one end and developed European economic circle at the other, and encompassing countries with huge potential for economic development. Under this vision, the speculations are raised mainly by the maritime component of the initiative, called the "21ˢᵗ Century Maritime Silk Road" or "21 世纪海上丝绸之路" (MSR). The MSR initiative was put forward by Chinese President Xi Jinping during his visit to Indonesia in October 2013, in order to deepen economic and maritime links. It came as an adjunct to Xi's first proposition of building the "Silk Road Economic Belt",[1] during his visit to Kazakhstan in September 2013.

Here, it is important to note, that China's mercantile rational of building economic activity along the sea lanes will automatically get translated in an increased military activity. That is, to say, the economic logic behind China's maritime silk road initiative is mainly driven by its strategic interest of security. Most importantly, with this initiative, China aims to build a maritime trade and transportation route reaching through the South China Sea and Indian Ocean to the eastern Mediterranean, encompassing South and Southeast Asia, East Africa, and the Near and Middle East. It is rather motivated by China's own strategic interests of expanding and strengthening its military presence in the strategic corridor of Indian Ocean along the Maritime Silk Road.

Given this security logic, the present paper argues that China's quest to build the "21ˢᵗ century maritime Silk Road" is the strategy to increase its military presence, especially along the

Indian Ocean region. This is driven by the security complex that China faces in the Indian Ocean, which is dominated by United States. This is also in complementary to China's 'Malacca Dilemma'—which severely challenges China's national interest of economic growth and development.

CHINA'S VISION OF THE 21ˢᵀ CENTURY MARITIME SILK ROAD: THE KEY OBJECTIVES

China's "New Silk Road" concept is rooted in history as there existed an overland Silk Route and a MSR that connected China to countries across Asia, Africa and Europe. Drawing from this past practice, China in recent years has built a network of highways and railroads from north to south and from east to less developed western and south western regions. With its achievement at the domestic level, China sees "an opportunity to link the hinterland with south Asia, Europe, Africa and even the Americas". [2]

Following up and concretising on President Xi Jinping's idea of deepening economic and maritime links through the land and sea routes, on 28 March 2015, during the Boao Forum for Asia, China's National Development and Reform Commission, in conjunction with China's Foreign Ministry and Commerce Ministry, issued an action plan for the Belt and Road, bringing the concept one important step closer to realisation. Titled the "Vision and Actions on Jointly Building Silk Road Economic Belt and 21ˢᵗ Century Maritime Silk Road", the official document lays out the basic goals of the "One Belt One Road" Initiative, as pointed:

> "It is aimed at promoting orderly and free flow of economic factors, highly efficient allocation of resources and deep integration of markets; encouraging the countries along the Belt and Road to achieve economic policy coordination and carry out broader and more in-depth regional cooperation of higher standards; and

jointly creating an open, inclusive and balanced regional economic cooperation architecture that benefits all". [3]

Specifically to MSR, in building the connectivity, the 'Vision Statement' notes that: "The Road is designed to go from China's coast to Europe through the South China Sea and the Indian Ocean in one route, and from China's coast through the South China Sea to the South Pacific in the other". [4] Wherein, the "Road" is a maritime network of port and other coastal infrastructure from South and Southeast Asia to East Africa and the northern Mediterranean Sea. [5]

Given this plan of action, one of the key objective of China is to break the connectivity bottlenecks in Asia and beyond, which has seriously hindered development in many developing countries. And China wants to do so by building roads, railways and ports in these countries. Critical of this grand vision, many scholars have argued that China's New Silk Road strategy is a Chinese version of the "Marshall Plan"—wherein China wants to use such initiatives to seek influence and even dominance in Asia. [6] It is argued so as for China, 'the belt and the road' provides opportunities to expand Chinese influence while also showcases Beijing's softer side. With its "win-win" equation, China can foster a softer image for itself while boosting its regional influence. [7]

On the contrary, opposing this view, Chinese scholars have denounced it by maintaining the policy of "Three Nos":non interference in the internal affairs of other nations; not to seek the so called 'sphere of influence'; and not to strive for hegemony or dominance equally applies to the "One Belt One Road" policy. [8] In concurrence, China's such a stand is also clearly reflected in the official position which dismisses the skepticism over the Chinese "Marshall Plan" motive. Keeping this view, the government document on "Visions and Actions", clearly posits that: "The Belt and Road Initiative is in line with the purposes and principles of the UN Charter" and "upholds the Five Principles of Peaceful Coexistence". It further states that the objective aims at:

> "[a] win-win cooperation that promotes common development and prosperity and a road towards peace and friendship by enhancing mutual understanding and trust, and strengthening all-round exchanges. The Chinese government advocates peace and cooperation, openness and inclusiveness, mutual learning and mutual benefit". [9]

That is to say, China's vision of building the network from Asia to Europe and Africa is based on an absolute calculus rather than a zero-sum based strategy of relative gains.

Thereby, having this broad objective to connect China to the outer world and vice-versa, MSR is representative of a next step to China's strategic development. That is, Beijing sees its geopolitical and security interests as best served by tying other countries into ever closer economic relationships. And in this case, the New Silk Road via the MSR will enhance China's economic and political clout complemented by a significant expansion of its military influence.

CHINA'S 21ˢᵀ CENTURY MARITIME SILK ROAD: STRATEGIC INTERESTS AND SECURITY CONCERNS

The rational behind the objective of 'breaking the connectivity bottlenecks' can be understood in the systemic challenges that restrict China's rise as a global player in the international player. This can be assessed in the growing security and strategic threats that severely challenge China's great power politics syndrome. Most importantly, this ideation is directly linked to President Xi Jinping's primary vision of "Chinese Dream"[10]—to realise "the great renewal of the Chinese nation"[11] by "making the country stronger through development". [12] In this view, China's MSR is a mechanism to fulfil the Chinese Dream, as this ambitious vision reflects Xi Jinping's thinking on "New Type of International Relations" and "New Type of relationship between Major Powers in the 21ˢᵗ century" with focus on "no conflict, no confrontation, mutual respect and win-win cooperation".[13] This can be said so, as the official statement of China posits that "the Chinese Dream is not the Chinese people dreaming of remaining behind closed doors, but a dream of opening up; a dream that China can collaborate with the world and achieve a win-win situation. The Chinese dream will benefit China and the world".[14] Drawing the link, it can be stated that China's ambition of MSR lies in fulfilling the Chinese Dream.

In this context, what makes MSR important in fulfilling the Chinese Dream is the rising concerns embedded in the challenges to China's national interest. That is, internally, China is faced with the "new normal" caused by its economic slowdown, compounded with a rising energy insecurity and also the domestic instabilities caused by Uyghur separatist actions in Xinjiang and others. While broadly the main concern revolves externally, around the 'US-factor', whereby, China faces a severe challenge to its expanding influence in the east by United States "pivot to Asia" policy—as US with its allies such as South Korea, Japan, Taiwan, Philippines, Australia and India aims to contain China in the Indo-pacific region.[15] For instance, economically US-driven trade agreements, such as the Trans-Pacific Partnership (TPP) and the Transatlantic Trade and Investment Partnership (TTIP) as well as the EU-Japan agreement show comprehensive liberalisation agendas but exclude China, and militarily, US security alliances with Japan, India, Vietnam, Philippines and others aim to constrain China's maritime activities. Under this broad framework of strategic concerns, Xi Jinping's MSR initiative provides a strategic survival tactic for China. What lies at the core is the key interest to fulfil its national security agenda by securing and safeguarding its economic growth by expanding its interest to the west and thus, further legitimising the Chinese Communist Party's rule in China.

In this perspective, in order to meet the domestic economic slowdown, infrastructure exports are designed to address the problem of overproduction at home.[16] While, given the central challenge of US "pivot to Asia" policy, China's active efforts to develop strategic and economic relationships along the Maritime Silk Road provides an opportunity for China to escape the growing containment and encirclement. To this view, some Chinese military authors have asserted to call the route of the Maritime Silk Road "the crucial strategic direction of China's rise" (中国崛起的关键战略方向), indicating a belief that developing the route will be critical to the country's entire development program.[17] What makes MSR a key driver can be assessed from China's security concerns. In the recent years, Chinese leadership under Xi Jinping have continually emphasised on China's primary security concern, which lies in the preservation of conditions conducive to continued economic development. According to Jiang Qianlin, "China's effort to build a middle-class society is entering a decisive stage under new historical conditions" during which external conditions could present a threat to larger social and economic development goals.[18] In safeguarding the interests, the strategic task of China's armed forces, as pointed in the 2015 Defence White Paper,[19] is to uphold a "holistic view of national security, balance internal and external security, homeland and citizen security, traditional and non-traditional security, subsistence and development security, and China's own security and the common security of the world", and thus, act as a "security guarantee for China's peaceful development. In pursuing China's national interest, the key task of the armed forces is to support China's efforts to diplomatically and economically tackle the "security dynamics along [the] periphery" (周边安全动态)—with the "periphery" encompassing states, islands, and sea lanes critical to China's lines of communication, especially in the East China Sea, South China Sea, and Indian Ocean.[20]

Given these strategic concerns and interests, China's Maritime Silk Road acts as a security network as it represents China's most vital sea lines of communication, both because it gives China access to three major economic zones (Southeast Asia, South Asia, and the Middle East) and because it is the route for many of China's strategic materials, including oil, iron ore, and copper ore imports.[21] This can be said so, as MSR begins at Fuzhou in Southeast China's Fuzhou province and heads south into the ASEAN nations, crosses Malacca Strait and turns west to countries along the Indian Ocean before meeting the land based Silk Road in Venice via the Red Sea and Mediterranean.[22] Under this ambit of maritime connectivity, China plans to build hard and soft infrastructure from Indo-Pacific to Africa, including transport, energy, water management, communication, earth monitoring, economic and social infrastructure.

In this view, one of China's primary interests lie in enhancing its foothold in the Indian Ocean. For with its longstanding entanglement in the territorial disputes of South and East China Sea, China's strategic focus in Indian Ocean suffered significant ignorance. What makes China to shift its focus is that in the recent decades, Indian Ocean, the third largest waterway in the world has surpassed the Atlantic and Pacific Oceans as the world's largest and most strategically significant maritime trade for global economy and security. With its strategic geographical landscape, the Indian Ocean Region (IOR) surrounded by Africa, Asia and Australia serves as a maritime highway linking transcontinental human and economic relationships. Thereby, making the Indian Ocean the new theatre of 'Great Power' politics of the twenty-first century. What makes Indian Ocean an important geopolitical hotspot is the fact that it contains the vital sea lanes—acting as a strategic trade corridor. For more than 80 per cent of the world's seaborne trade in oil transits through Indian Ocean choke points, with 40 per cent passing through the Strait of Hormuz, 35 per cent through the Strait of Malacca and 8 per cent through the Bab el-Mandab Strait.[23]

In this strategic calculus, it becomes imperative for any great power to strengthen its presence in the Indian Ocean region (IOR). In this view, China adds no exception given this logic. Unlike United States and India, China witnesses a 'pariah' status in the IOR given its lack of geographical proximity as well as logistical support base. Facing this strategic disadvantage, it has become imperative for China to safeguard its economic and security interests in the Indian Ocean. And in doing so, China needs to strengthen its military presence and activities in the Indian Ocean in order to safeguard its interests from the challenges imposed, especially at the chokepoints in the strategic sea lanes of communication. Hence, MSR helps to obtain this objective by securing China's interests by building a security network through ports, infrastructure facilities and importantly, strategic military bases.

CHINA AND THE 21ˢᵀ CENTURY MARITIME SILK ROAD: POLICIES AND ACTIONS

Under its economic logic, China led Asian Infrastructure Investment Bank (AIIB) and the New Silk Road Fund (NSRF), have been established to provide financial support for the New Silk Road strategy. Of which, with the vision of building network, under the sea-route strategy of MSR, China has already financed new ports in the Indian Ocean in Bangladesh (Chittagong), Myanmar (Sittwe), Pakistan (Gwadar) and Sri Lanka (Hambantota). While the primary focus is mainly to seek commercial benefits, but China in parallel is also building naval power in order to safeguard its maritime trade routes. Most importantly, the sea route will serve China's core interests in the South China Sea, where China faces a severe threat—"Malacca Dilemma" at the Straits of Malacca—a strategic choke point to China's free flow of trade and energy supplies along the Sea Lanes of Communication.

Beijing with its MSR, is seeking to co-opt strategically located states in an economic and security alliance led by it, is working specifically to acquire naval-access outposts through agreements for refuelling, replenishment, crew rest and maintenance. Its efforts involve gaining port projects along vital sea lanes of communication, securing new supplies of natural resources, and building energy and transportation corridors to China through Myanmar and Pakistan. In this light, at sea, the initiative aims at jointly building smooth, secure and efficient transport routes connecting major sea ports along the Maritime Silk Road. In this case, the China-Pakistan Economic Corridor (CPEC) and the Bangladesh-China-India-Myanmar Economic Corridor are closely related to the overall Belt and Road Initiative.[24]

Under the "21st Century Silk Road", the policy for China is to build new port infrastructure that links to inland transport networks, increase the number of international sea routes, improve logistics (including through enhanced usage of information technology), dismantle trade and investment barriers and deepen financial integration by greater usage of the renminbi.[25] Putting the vision into action, China's sea route buildup under MSR has taken roots with the financing of $ 46 billion investment in Pakistan, in building the 3000 km, long CPEC, which would connect the Arabian Sea port of Gwadar in southwestern Pakistan with the Xinjiang region of northwestern China. What makes CPEC important under MSR is that Gwadar, as China views is a potential hub for trade with the Middle East, Africa and Europe. The project will also promote the development in Xinjiang and Tibet.[26] This project makes Pakistan the central link between the maritime and overland Silk Roads. Besides CPEC, in September 2015, China called for a fuller economic integration with the Association of the South East Asian Nations (ASEAN), with the enforcement of the Nanning-Singapore Economic Corridor under the framework of the Maritime Silk Road.[27]

Moreover, in addition to Pakistan, another channel through which China has sought to win influence in the Indian Ocean Rim is Sri Lanka. It signed major contracts with Sri Lanka's former President, Mahinda Rajapaksa, to turn that country—located along major shipping lanes—into a major stop on the Chinese nautical "road",[28] by means of Hambantota and Colombo Port City projects. China and Malaysia have already announced a joint port project in Malacca.[29] While in the recent attempt, on 26 November, 2015, Beijing confirmed its plans to build the first overseas naval military base in the East African nation of Djibouti—which overlooks the narrow Bab el-Mandab Straits. This channel, separating Africa from the Arabian Peninsula and constituting one of the busiest shipping lanes in the world, leads into the Red Sea and north to the Mediterranean.

This expansion clearly reflects the military intention under MSR. For Djibouti military base will provide China capabilities to respond to contingencies affecting freedom of navigation in and around the Persian Gulf—which is mainly controlled by the United States.[30] Most importantly, by having its military base in Indian Ocean, China can expand its naval capabilities in terms of developing sea denial capabilities comprising of deployment of submarines in Indian Ocean and strategic anti access/area denial (A2/AD) capabilities.[31] The Chinese maneuvering activities in the Indian Ocean clarify China's larger plan to project power in the Middle East,

Africa and Europe—which aims to challenge America's authority and counter India's natural-geographic advantage.[32] These Chinese projects and activities aim at carving out an important role for China in the Indian Ocean through his Maritime Silk Road initiative.

Thereby, from the above policies adopted by China under the vision of building the "21st Century Maritime Silk Road", it is clear that it is a multi-pronged strategy that involves economic, diplomatic and military interests. Here, it is important to note that, with MSR, China's real intentions lie in securing the sea route to secure its global power status and thereby, challenge the US-led order. That is, an important strategic step forward in fulfilling the dream of "rejuvenation of the Chinese nation".

CONCLUSION

Given China's assertive actions of land reclamation activities in the South China Sea to that of recently building its first overseas base in Djibouti, it can be strongly posited that maritime domain has become the key aspect of China's foreign policy, wherein China wants to play the great power game of 21st century. Under a commercial and mercantile framework, Beijing's benign intentions of overseas investments and aid policy is in reality motivated by the goal of turning the economic rational into a strategic weight. it can be said so, as the MSR's infrastructure buildup is mainly aimed at key littoral states that run along the trade route, in order to guarantee China's maritime security along the critical SLOCs. The way MSR is being shaped it can be clearly stated that it is mainly a security strategy. Undoubtedly, the grand project to deepen economic and maritime links is mainly about expanding and securing China's maritime routes to the Middle East and beyond through the Indian Ocean, which acts as the bridge between Asia and Europe. Therefore, China's "21st Century Maritime Silk Road" is a survival strategy for China, aimed at securing its economic and strategic interests by building its strategic clout through maritime links that connect Asia to Europe and Africa—strategically connecting China to the world and vice-versa.

REFERENCES

[1] The "Silk Road Economic Belt" comprises the land route focuses on bringing together China, Central Asia, Russia and Europe (the Baltic), linking China with the Persian Gulf and the Mediterranean Sea through Central Asia and West Asia, and connecting China with Southeast Asia, South Asia and the Indian Ocean.

[2] Deepak, B.R., "One Belt One Road": China at the Centre of the Global Geopolitics and Geo-economics," *South Asia Analysis*, Paper No. 5838, December 4, 2014.

[3] National Development and Reform Commission, Ministry of Foreign Affairs, and Ministry of Commerce of the People's Republic of China, "Vision and Actions on Jointly Building Silk Road Economic Belt and 21ˢᵗ-Century Maritime Silk Road," March 28, 2015.

[4] Ibid.

[5] "The One Belt, One Road Initiatives," *Maritime Insight*, Issue 1, June 2015.

[6] Dingding, Chen, "China's 'Marshall Plan' is much more," *The Diplomat*, November 10, 2014.

[7] Tiezzi, Shannon, "The New Silk Road: China's Marshall Plan?," *The Diplomat*, November 6, 2014.

[8] Zi, Shi, ""One Road & One Belt" New Thinking With Regard to Concepts and Practice," Lecture delivered at the 30ᵗʰ anniversary of Conference of the Schiller Institute, Germany, October 14, 2014.

[9] *Op. cit.* "Vision and Actions," March 28, 2015.

[10] The vision of zhongguo meng or "Chinese Dream" was first spelled by Xi Jinping on 29 November 2012, in his keynote speech at his visit to the National Historical Museum's Exhibition on "The Road to Revival" in Beijing, pledging to fulfil the goal of "great renewal of the Chinese nation".

[11] "Xi pledges "Great Renewal of with Chinese Nation"," *Xinhuanet, November 29, 2012.*

[12] Rajan, D.S., "China: Can Xi Jinping's "Chinese Dream" Vision be realized?," *C3S*, Paper No. 2052, January 2, 2014.
[13] Ibid.
[14] Ibid.
[15] Lo, Chi, "China's "One Belt One Road": The Land and Sea Strategies (Part 2 of 2)," *BNP Paribas*, July 8, 2015.
[16] Chellaney, Brahma, "China's Indian Ocean Strategy," *The Japan Times*, June 23, 2015.
[17] Clemens, Morgan, "The Maritime Silk Road and the PLA," A Paper for "China as a Maritime Power" Conference, CNA Conference Facility, Arlington-Virginia, July 28–29, 2015.
[18] Ibid.
[19] Ministry of National Defense of the People's Republic of China, "China's Military Strategy," The State Council Information Office of the People's Republic of China, May 26, 2015.
[20] Morgan Clemens, "The Maritime Silk Road and the PLA".
[21] Ibid.
[22] Deepak, B.R., "One Belt One Road": China at the Centre of the Global Geopolitics and Geo-economics," *South Asia Analysis*, Paper No. 5838, December 4, 2014.
[23] DeSilva-Ranasinghe, Sergei, "Why the Indian Ocean Matters," *The Diplomat*, March 02, 2011.
[24] *Op. Cit.* "Vision and Actions," March 28, 2015.
[25] Lo, Chi, "China's "One Belt One Road": The Land and Sea Strategies (Part 2 of 2)," *BNP Paribas*, July 8, 2015, p. 6.
[26] Janjua, Haroon, "Transport project with China could boost economy," *Nikkei Asian Review*, December 24, 2015.
[27] Aneja, Atul, "Lure of Nanning-Singapore Economic Corridor Could Help Ease South China Sea Tensions," *The Hindu*, September 19, 2015.
[28] Chellaney, Brahma, June 23, 2015.
[29] Yale, William, "China's Maritime Silk Road Gamble," *The Diplomat*, April 22, 2015.
[30] Brewster, David, "China's First Overseas Military Base in Djibouti Likely to be a Taste of Things to Come," *The Interpreter*, December 2, 2015.
[31] Jash, Amrita, "China in Djibouti: Setting the Strategic Foot in Indian Ocean Region," *IndraStra Global*, December 17, 2015.
[32] Chellaney, Brahma, June 23, 2015.

Geostrategic Impact of the Rise of China in the Asia-Pacific Region

Radha Raghuramapatruni

ABSTRACT

The, Asia Pacific region has emerged as a significant strategic centre in international political affairs. The region's dependence on Sea Lines of Communication and the proximity with a rising China has hoisted its stature in US policy calculus whose focus will now shift to this region once the planned withdrawal of its forces takes place by the end of 2014. The rise of China has created many ripples in the international relations not only regionally but globally too. This raises a question on how to measure the China's rise which has become focal point for today's international politics in common. A question about "whether a rising China is a threat" could be measured in terms of three aspects—Capability, intention and image. The geographical space which has the potential to create geopolitical disturbances across the world is the South China Sea in Asia Pacific. In this context the current paper would discuss the geostrategic impact of the rise of China in the Asia-Pacific Region.

INTRODUCTION

The emergence of Asia Pacific region as a new strategic centre in the international political landscape is now a reality. The region occupies a huge area starting from the Indian subcontinent to the west coast of America. It spans two oceans, the Pacific and the Indian, busy pathways of maritime activity and strategy. The region is home to about half of the world population. It has a number of important centres, of world economy whose goods, tools and services are competing with ways. Asia Pacific thus provides both a competitive edge and an economic challenge to the West.

Three of the most important straits—Malacca Strait, Sunda Strait and the Strait of Lombok—are situated in the region. The Malacca Strait is the world's busiest shipping lane equivalent to Suez or Panama. Almost all the shipping passes through these three straits which further signifies the strategic importance of this region for regional and international actors. Three regional littoral states Indonesia, Malaysia and Singapore are adjacent to these choke points and thus have the potential to exercise control over a significant percentage of the world's maritime trade.

Apart from dependence on the Sea Lines of Communications (SLOC), the proximity with China has raised the region's stature in US policy calculus. Therefore, US's prime aim is to counter the emerging predominance of an Asian power— China whose rapid progress has the potential to challenge US supremacy in the world. The US along with her allies, particularly Japan, South Korea and Australia, wants to "encircle" China. US's recent growing politico-military as well as economic ties with the ASEAN states are also marked to weakening China's growing ingress in Southeast Asia. The US-India strategic alliance is also a step in this direction, wherein both the countries view China as a potential challenger, for US at global level and India at regional level.

The 19th century was the century of Europe and the 20th century was that of America. With the advent of the 21st century several analysts have suggested it was now the turn of Asia to lead the world in international politics. It is viewed that the extraordinary chemistry of demography, the significant function of the state and the recent economic progress will take Asia frontward. It is assumed the next theatre would be Asia Pacific, where the future would be played out, where the world would see the involvement of major powers like United States of America, China, Russia, Australia, the European Union and India in a state of competition when their interests collide. In this context the current paper discusses the geostrategic impact of the rise of China in the Asia-Pacific Region.

OBJECTIVES OF THE STUDY

1. To analyse the geostrategic importance of the rise of China in the Asia Pacific Region.
2. To assess the military, strategic and economic implication of the rise of China in the Asia Pacific Region.

CHINA EMERGED AS A MAJOR GEO-ECONOMIC PLAYER IN EAST ASIA

China in the 1970's from the edge of collapse has travelled to reach to the centre stage of world economic development. China's rise together with the recent global financial crisis scholars have started questioning the very existence of the notion of 'Washington Consensus' and at the same time about the emergence of the 'Beijing Consensus' (Horesh, 2015). Rise of China has once again brought the logic of geo-economic vs. geo-politics at the forefront especially in the Asia Pacific region (Luttwak, 2011).

Geo-economic which can be simply put as the economic consequences of geopolitical trends and national power have seems to be gradually come to dominate the World geopolitical system. According to Sanjay Baru (2012). Whether notion of "trade follows the flag" (meaning economic consequences of projection of national power) or 'the flag follows trade' (meaning geopolitical consequences of essentially economic phenomena) would eventually both be the outcome of geo-economics.

Historically, till the end of Cold War, politics remained the core of state matter, and geopolitics was largely an element of ideology rather than economic element. So this was the reason that all the important ideas which defined the present geo-economics emanated almost after the end of Cold War.

On the idea of geo-economics next important to Kennedy was Edward Luttwak. His work on "From Geopolitics to Geo-economics: Logic of Conflict, Grammar of Commerce', highlights the importance of Geo-economic in the 21st century. Barring few states which are historically and culturally inactive like Myanmar and Switzerland, the desirable scope of geo-economic activism by the state is already becoming the focal point of political debate and partisan controversy (Luttwak, 2011).

After the end of Cold War, despite Japan being large economy, and reaching its zenith in the 1980s, having a top class technology-cum-manufacturing sector, could not convert those strengths into geopolitical influence, let alone leadership. This difference is explained by Jonquieres, (2012), who argues that economy size do not, of itself, confer international influence.

But this is not the case when China got similar opportunity; it translated into matching geopolitical strength and the rise of China is quite visible. May be this is because of different historical and cultural background. China still has the memory of humiliation intact which it faced during 'Open door Policy'. Rise of China is quite different from Japan, not in line with Western model. China tries to set the international order according to its own rule. This is evident in the recent est-blishment of New Development Bank, Asian Infrastructure Investment Bank (AIIB), 'One Belt One Road' policy under land based and maritime trade silk route.

Unlike in the past China is no more ready to be taught by those who once treated it as a pariah state. But now those developed state have started looking to China for bail out. China's accomplishment in saving out US from Global financial crisis says that why the "Beijing Consensus" has attracted so many admirers in recent years. As beautifully pointed out by him' in World Economic Forum (WEF) in Davos, usually the Swiss resort used to be filled with various scholars, celebrity, politicians. Beyond this Jiabao openly blamed the west for this financial crisis.

Few years ago in the light of established 'Washington Consensus' this was almost unthinkable. However, after the global meltdown and its adverse impact on major western economies and the unaffected Chinese economy, world recognised the rising China in terms of its economic growth as 'Beijing Consensus'. Further after the world financial crisis (2008), this gave China an opportunity to assert at World level. It was the first time when a non-Western country is on the way asserting over the trans-Atlantic World.

The last APEC summit in Beijing on Nov. 2014 again proved China as a geo-economic power. Beijing came out looking very much what it is touted to be—the world's second largest economy—now leading the charge towards a freely-trading region known as the Free Trade Area of the Asia Pacific (FTAAP). For a pariah economy that was not even part of the global trading system, this is one giant leap. Though FTAAP is not a Chinese idea but excitingly Beijing saw the renewal of APEC as a major stage for regional economic integration led by China.

GEOSTRATEGIC IMPACT OF THE RISE OF CHINA FOR ASIA PACIFIC

Rise of China has created many ripples in international relations not only regionally but globally too. This raises one question on how to measure the China's rise which has become focal point for today's international politics in common, put this in another simple way, as question about "whether a rising China is a threat". This suggests that it should be measured in terms of three aspects—Capability, intention, strategy, and image. There are few geographical spaces which has the potential to create geopolitical disturbances across the world.

SOUTH CHINA SEA: THEATRE OF GREAT POWERS

The South China Sea is a marginal sea that is part of the Pacific Ocean, encompassing an area from the Singapore and Malacca Straits to the Strait of Taiwan of around 3,5000,000 square kilometres. Its importance lies in various parameters namely, its Sea lanes of communication (SLOC), its strategic aspect and related claims by number of nearby sovereign countries, hidden mineral resources, rich fishing resources, etc.

SCS in Asia Pacific owes its significance due to its geostrategic location which affects countries both—directly and indirectly. It is surrounded by Southeast Asian (SEA) countries, Strait of Malacca in South West, Southern China and Taiwan in north it is considered by Robert Kaplan (2014) as like a 'cork' in the bottle of South China Sea. The Indian Ocean holds the major transportation zone across which billions of dollars of oil and cargo goods ferry between Atlantic to Pacific. All the hydrocarbon from middle East comes by super tanker across the Indian Ocean, crosses Malacca, goes up through SCS to Japan, South Korea and China. In fact SCS handles much of the commercial traffic of three powers—China, Japan and South Korea making it significant geostrategic location of the world.

SOUTH CHINA SEA: GEOSTRATEGIC COMPETENCE

Many scholars criticise China over its intentions on South China Sea (SCS). Robert Kaplan logically explains the issue by comparing both the major great powers intention by comparing geopolitics of two major seas-Caribbean and South

China Seas respectively. Robert Kaplan, (2014) by cited the views of a Chinese Colonel "China is doing nothing unusual in SCS that the American did not do in greater Caribbean in the 19th century and 20th century. Why should we be different? US after settling down in temperate Continental North America tried to control over its blue water adjacent to land mass in the greater Caribbean Sea and Gulf Mexico. So once US got controlled over Caribbean it got control over strategic hemisphere and that was the story of 20th century".

China following the dominance of US had in Caribbean, had instituted what they called 'Cow tongue'—the nine dash line, to claim their control of the South China Sea (SCS) maritime space. Based on US domination over Caribbean Sea and subsequently leading to the domination over Western Hemisphere and eventually to World domination some scholar's question how do US would view if similar intention of China comes over its SCS domination and then subsequently over the domination of Eastern Hemisphere. Over this question Kaplan says as the Chinese sees the SCS as unlocking the door to breaking out of first Island chain of Pacific into the wider Pacific and also allowing them to envelope to encircle Taiwanese sovereignty without actually having to conquer Taiwan. It actually means surround by more and more trade. Air connections, more and more ballistic missile focused on it at the same time.

And most importantly as Kaplan (2014) considers SCS as the anti-chamber to the Indian Ocean where China is building or helping to finance its modern deep water port all along as part of their emerging commercial empire. So if the China could gain in SCS and unlock the world to them, it actually would be able to unlock most of maritime territories in Western Hemisphere to them. In the way the Caribbean unlock the world for US. If that happens does that mean threat to US?

Many Scholars say yes, because US always had the advantage of balance of power in Asia Pacific. But US cannot go on to dominate in future, the kind of dominance that it exercised in post WW II, because in those period there was no Chinese, Japanese and other emerging power navy development. All the small countries like Philippine, Vietnam are busy in their internal problems. All this is changed now and still changing. There are advanced military building going up in Asia Pacific region. The region is emerging in multi-polar power but easier was American unipolar based. Thus, there has been a shift.

MILITARY AND STRATEGIC INFLUENCE OF RISING CHINA IN THE REGION

The twenty-first century Asia Pacific is being challenged by new emerged geopolitical situation largely of rising China. This has led to United States and China themselves engaged in a 'range war in the western Pacific, a competition has come to occupied over the China's growing military technological capabilities and the subsequent responses by the regional powers like US and others. China's military capability has enhanced much in the past sixty years. Unlike, in the past for instance in 1996 during the Taiwan Crisis, when US displayed its forces which led Chine to go back foot. But in just eleven years afterwards, according to a study from RAND informed that the US military could lose to Peoples Liberation Army (PLA) of China.

China's current force structure provides effective defence against any effort to invade and seize Chinese territory. Since China considers the South China Sea as "China Lake" overriding other countries sovereign claim over the Sea. This endangers Vietnam's national and economic security. Further China's strategic assertiveness over the high seas of SCS like as it did through the sudden announcement Air Defence Identification Zone (ADIZ) over East Sea leading to criticism from Japan, US, Australia and other countries. Such Chinese assertiveness can be expected in future over SCS too.

ECONOMIC INFLUENCE OF RISING CHINA IN THE REGION

China sitting over huge wealth and investment capability has developed potential to influence the foreign policies of regional countries like Vietnam and Australia and others. Small countries like Vietnam which due to its asymmetric relationship with China has no option but to share its growing regional maritime security problem with powers like US, India, Japan and others. As consequences to the Vietnam and other regional countries effort of balancing Chinese assertiveness, Chinese media commentaries warned that such nations siding with extra-territorial powers like United States in the Asia-Pacific will be penalised economically, while calling for Chinese "countermeasures" to the US military build-up in the region. Further some strategic analysts talk of China's ability to outspend the US to defend its Asia-Pacific interest.

China's trade ties with and economic influence in Asia pacific neighbours is greater than ever. Further in recent years China has established many regional financial institutions like Asian Infrastructure Investment Bank (AIIB), Regional Comprehensive Economic Partnership (RCEP), which no doubt has attracted many regional and western global countries and many have even become founding members of the AIIB.

To enhance its trade and economic ties and eventually integrate the regional economies China has started negotiations for Silk Road Economic Belt and 21st Century maritime Silk Road, establishing land and sea routes linking Asia, Eastern Europe and Africa. The two projects have become popular as 'One Belt, One Road' system.

China's "Belt and Road initiatives "are really about economic integration of Asia with the Chinese economy and the emerging Asian market, and by joining in and shaping the alignment of the rail, road, sea routes and gas pipelines India can become a node for Western and South Asia.

Including a services component in the projects will add to their productivity and support cooperation between the Asian giants; trade is a win-win proposition.

GEOPOLITICAL IMPLICATION OF CHINA'S RISE IN THE REGION

The growth of China has brought about new undercurrents in the Asian geopolitics and security, particularly in the past two decades. One frequently reads about China's growing assertiveness from its growing economic-politico strength, as well as a strong perception of US at bargaining position. China's growing power play a key role in generating new dynamics in Asian regional security and geo-political environment.

China is not an ordinary nation. It is a great power by design. Once China develops, the eternal impact of its development will be extraordinary. The most significant external impact of China's rise is the consequential pressure it places on the onset of a power transition between China and the United State, the essence of which concerns both the current international system and the future of international relations.

Some predict that China will continue to press change to the US led international order and initiate a confrontation with the United State and its allies. There are several key reasons for this expectation. Like as historically a known fact that every rising powers tried to become a dominant power. Further China being a closed political system its very hard to predict its future course of action especially as it is getting more and more wealthy. And eventually considering its potentialities on the basis of its past and present status china seems to have the capacity and potential to become a superpower, possibly eclipsing the United Sates in the future.

Thus, in view of all of the above conditions and apparently more, the "China threat" is the cause of great concern for US and its allied in Asia. Also the China's neighbouring countries which share territorial and maritime conflict with China perceived similar threat.

CHINA'S RISE AND ITS ECONOMIC IMPACT ON THE REGION

As many scholars' points out that as on one hand, US have started shrinking and on other hand, China has started expanding its influence over Asia Pacific. Impact of China rise has long been felt by the US administration. As a consequences, Obama since the beginning of his term has paid significant attention to East Asia and its regional multilateral institutions like EAS, ASEAN+6 and others. US better understands that the East Asian regional and Asia Pacific over all stands vital for its economic growth, which at present is largely being challenged by Chinese twenty-first century established economic 'hub-and spoke' system. This is the time when Europe too is facing bad situation in economic growth.

Nevertheless, US and EU economies are still the two main pillars of trans-Atlantic trade and commerce which constitutes of about fifty percent of world GDP. Thus as a consequence in order to gain and consolidate its loosing economic space US has started talking about Trans Pacific Partnership (TPP). Similar to this US has started another scheme called Transatlantic Trade and Investment partnership (TTIP) with European Union to unravel prospect for American citizens and businesses, and farmers through increased accessibility to European markets for Made-in-America goods and services, for which there has been huge outcry going on in Europe. This will help to promote US.

With respect to transpacific partnership, China was deliberately excluded from this free trade agreement which US is negotiating with states along Pacific Rim. According to Gertken, (2013). View TPP is to look how US has traditionally tried its vast economy as tool for influence across the world. And in particular a looking at the Pacific major economies like Japan and China and number of other emerging economy and Southeast Asia. In the region US wants to create a framework across the Asia Pacific which will then be a framework for any future being regional trade liberalization initiatives.

So notably China was left out of TPP and where the US has a kind of saying and at the same time they would have an ambitious agenda, where they would seek more than just trading in goods where China can dominate and get into area where US is great which have to do with things like services, investments and all kinds of deeper structural issues.

US wants to create that king of framework, one that, where it can go forward in future working with their partners and when China joins it latter would have to agree with all the rules and regulations. And at least that's the hope for US.

Similarly, Taneja (2014) quoted that the intention "United State" original logic of US-pivot to Asia is to maintain its prevailing dominant position in Asian Pacific. And taking advantage of region's economic dynamism through the free trade economy with the support of Trans Pacific Partnership (TPP) because there is strategic thinking behind that once the deal is done, and then invite China to become a member of its After that is done and when China is allowed to join TPP which is already has took its shape, then China will have to accept all its terms and conditions. Then China will not be a party to the agreement—called as Regional Economic

Co-operation Partnership (RECP) linking the Asia Pacific region with its economic system for in search enhanced economic growth.

Further, China's high profile hosting of the APEC meetings and its active role in the establishment of the AIIB as well as its plan to promote the Silk Road belt economy are a sign of the country's deeper involvement in regional affairs. If that is achieved, trade tariffs would be reduced across the Asia Pacific economic region, promoting regional economic cooperation and prosperity. As the world's second largest economy and a major player in the Asia Pacific Region, China has seen its ever expanding economic influence benefiting its neighbours and the region as a whole through generating business and trade opportunities and contributing to regional growth. However, some have wrongfully construed China's rise as a threat to their influence in the region.

These great power economic gimmicks in Asia pacific, represents both opportunity and challenges for the regional countries. Depending on different their perceptions, different responses are bound to emerge. In particular the responses of Vietnam and Australia will be analysed. Definitely, East Asian countries are lured by the economic growth of China and want to get benefited out of it but at the same time are also cautious of China's economic influence.

There have been diverse views about the rising China, quite more are critical; some take it as a 'Threat'. However, Fend and He (2012), have quite benign view about recent change in China's foreign policy. They consider it as normal for rising China, to be assertive because of its changed national interest. They argue that China is quire right when it tries to bargain with US and other regional powers like Japan or Australia to satisfy its national interests. China returning to its zenith of glory is natural it would seek its share in the international system.

INDIA AS POTENTIAL "COUNTERWEIGHT" TO CHINA

With these developments taking place, an effort appears to be underway by the US to attract India to play a more pro-active role in South East Asia. In July 2011, Secretary Clinton during her major policy speech in Chennai, titled "India and the United States: A Vision for the 21st Century", citing a whole range of common economic and strategic interests, urged "India not to just look east, but to engage East and act East." Among other things, Secretary Clinton stressed the importance of India and the US working in concert to shape the regional agenda and the evolving architecture in East Asia. She declared that America wanted to include India and other partners to establish the ESA into the Asia Pacific's leading forum for dealing with matters relating to politics and security. She added that the United States desired to use ESA to help set American priorities and layout a vision for other regional institutes. While discussing India's growing role in the Asia Pacific and in South and Central Asia, she noted: "Yes it is ambitious agenda, but we can afford to be ambitious, because when we in the United States and particularly in the Obama Administration look at India, we see, as President Obama said, a nation that is not simply emerging, but has emerged, and a nation with whom we share so many bonds, and one that will be a leader globally in shaping the future we will all inherit. The latest decision of the United States to declare India as the linchpin in her new Asia Pacific strategy is not a new development. Actually it is an extension of her old strategy towards India. Several new initiatives have been announced consistent with the evolving approach. India is indirectly reinforcing US position on South China Sea by making the "safety and security" of maritime commerce in the Indian Ocean a key theme in its official rhetoric.

A new trilateral forum—US, India and Japan has been constituted. Earlier, former Australian Foreign Minister Kevin Rudd claimed a trilateral (US-Australia-India) security and economic initiative, though India has denied any knowledge of such a proposal. In addition India has already concluded "strategic partnership" with Japan and South Korea. All this does not necessarily mean that India is able, ready and willing e worked to help make it a reality." Because of its economic growth and strategic position in the Indian Ocean and the Malacca Strait areas, India is seen as a key partner in the new American strategy towards Asia Pacific. India is also worried about China's challenge to free entrance to the waters of South China Sea. Furthermore, Indian curiosity to get benefits from Vietnam's energy sources puts it in direct clash with China's claims over the territory. Although, India looks favourably towards America's new strategy towards Asia Pacific, owing to its own concerns about an assertive and militarily powerful China, yet it has so far been seen as an inactive observer amid increasing oceanic tensions and territorial disputes in the region. The degree and pace of Indian involvement in the US strategy would, however, be defined by the considerations of India's own strategic interests in the region and China's behaviour towards her border dispute and Indian priorities in the immediate neighbourhood.

CONCLUSION

In sum, Asia Pacific region is emerging as a new focal point both economically and strategically. Major Powers of the world have been struggling to excel in the region and get maximum benefits. The manifold strategic, diplomatic, security, and other initiatives by the US in the region display the most important shift in the international and regional dynamics of modern times. It is early to say whether we are seeing the beginning of Cold War II in Asia Pacific, albeit with different protagonists. Only time will tell how far India will be able to play its expected role as a "balancer" vis-à-vis China. However, these emerging trends would have deep implications for the regional order. Presently, what is clear is that the geopolitical landscape is getting more complex and complicated with both challenges and opportunities and major focal point has become China.

REFERENCES

[1] Akram, M. (2011) "Reversing Strategic 'Shrinkage'", pp. 283–304 in Pakistan: Beyond the 'Crisis State 'edited by Maliha Lodhi. Karachi: Oxford University Press.

[2] Baker, R. and Zhang, Z. (17 July 2012). "The Paradox of China's Naval Strategy", Stratfor: Global Intelligence. Available from: http://www.stratfor.com/weekly/paradox-chinas-naval-strategy [Accessed 17 July 2012]

[3] Bijian, Z. (2005). China's Peaceful Rise: Speeches of Zheng Bijian 1997–2005, Washington D.C.: Brookings Institute Press.

[4] Brzezinski, Z. (2012). Strategic Vision: America and the Crisis of Global Power; Basic Books.

[5] Brzezinski, Z. (1998). The Grand Chessboard: American Primacy and its Geostrategic Imperatives, Basic Books.

[6] Centre for Strategic and International Studies (CSIS), (2011). "What Does the Arab Spring Mean for Russia, Central Asia, and the Caucasus?" A Report of the CSIS Russia and Eurasia Program, edited by Aigerim Zikibayeva, September 2011.

[7] Pilling, David, "How America Should Adjust to the Pacific Century", Financial Times, November 16, 2011, (accessed February 4, 2012),

[8] Engdahl, F.W. (April, 2012). "Eurasian Economic Boom and Geopolitics: China's Land Bridge to Europe: The China-Turkey High-Speed Railway", 27 April 2012.

[9] Luttwak, Edward N. (2011). "The Rise of China vs. the Logic of Strategy", The Harvard University Press.

[10] Friedman, G. (2009). The Next 100 Years: A Forecast for the 21st Century, New York: Anchor Books.

[11] Hailin, Y. (2008). "China and South Asia Relations in a New Perspective" Institute of Asia Pacific Studies, Chinese Academy of Social Sciences.

[12] Niv, Horesh (2015). "Superpower, China? Historicizing Beijing's New Narratives of Leadership and East Asia's Response Thereto, World Scientific.

[13] Warimann, H.B., "South East Asian Armed Forces Modernize to Counter China Threat Perception," Asian Defence Journal (April 2012).

[14] Hillary Rodham Clinton, "America's Pacific Century", Foreign Policy.com, November 10, 2011, (accessed February 4, 2012), http://www.foreignpolicy.com/articles/2011/10/11/am

[15] Jonquières, Guy de (2012). China's geo-economics strategy: what power shift to China? IDEAS reports—special reports, Kitchen, Nicholas (ed.) SR012. LSE IDEAS, The London School of Economics and Political Science, London, UK.

[16] Kissinger, H. (2012). On China. Penguin Books. Kocaman, A. (2012), "The Arab Spring versus Inertia in Central Asia and the Caucasus", The Washington Review of Turkish and Eurasian Affairs, March, 2012.

[17] Lillis, J. (2012). "Will there be a Central Asian Spring?" Foreign Policy, 26 January 2012.

[18] Luttwak, 2011(2011). "The Rise of China vs. the Logic of Strategy", Harvard University Press, USA.

[19] Muckenhuber, D. (2013). "Why Has the Arab Spring Skipped Central Asia (So Far)?" Global Observatory: Analysis on Global Issues.

[20] Ramos, J.C. (2004). The Beijing Consensus. Foreign Policy Centre.

[21] Kaplan, Robert D. (2014). 'The South China Sea is to China what the Greater Caribbean was to the United States.

[22] Sanger, D.E. (2012). Confront and Conceal: Obama's Secret Wars and Surprising Use of American Power. New York: Crown Publishers.

[23] Saunders, P.C. (2006). "China's Global Activism: Strategy, Drivers, and Tools", Institute for National Strategic Studies Occasional Paper 4, Washington D.C.: National Defense University Press.

[24] Stockholm International Peace Research Institute (2012), SIPRI Year Book 2012: Armaments, Disarmaments and International Security.

[25] Baru, Sanjaya (2012). Merkel in China, Project Syndicate.

[26] The Christian Science Monitor (2011). "South Asian Spring?" The Monitor's View by the Monitor's Editorial Board, 27 July 2011.

[27] The Department of Defense, The Government of the United States of America (2012) Sustaining U.S. Global Leadership: Priorities for 21st Century Defense, Author.

[28] Tzu, S. (1988). The Art of War translated by Thomas Cleary, Boston and London: Shambhala Publications. United Nations Office on Drugs and Crime (2010), World Drug Report 2010, Author.

[29] World Bank (2012). World Development Indicators 2012, Author: Washington D.C.

[30] Wang, Zheng, "American Conspiracy: Strategic Suspicion and US Reengagement", The National Bureau of Asian Research, Asia Policy no.12, July 2011, (accessed February 5, 2012).

Geosrategic Interests of China in Eurasia: Imperatives for India

ABSTRACT

China has emerged as a leading economic power in the Indian Ocean Region (IOR) and South China Sea. China has established firm relations with many littoral members of IOR with its soft power diplomacy. It made huge inroads in many countries of the Asian Region in trade. Chinese companies invested upto US $ 30 billion by 2013 in ASEAN countries and China—ASEAN trade reached US $ 500 billion in 2015. China's geopolitical interests are positively seen heading a new direction in current era. Beijing is reaching out to near and distant neighbours in all directions of the globe and expanding its relationship with small and big countries. The proposed land based Silk Road Economic Belt (SREB) - an initiative of connectivity and cooperation among countries along Central Asia, West Asia, Middle East, towards Europe; and the new Maritime Silk Road (MSR) aiming to foster investments and collaboration along South China Sea, Western Pacific till Northern Africa-together called 'One Belt, One Road' (OBOR) are rapidly taking shape. The China-Pakistan Economic Corridor (CPEC), Rail links like 'New Eurasian Land Bridge' from Yiwu in China to Madrid in Europe, indicate China's extending focus towards Europe, through Central Asia and Eurasia. What began as 'March West' policy of Beijing is now transforming into a multifaceted network of economic, political and diplomatic relations with various nations. Recently China has signed 51 agreements with Pakistan, 31 related to CPEC, committing to invest US $ 46 billion; got contracts worth US $ 30 billion and US $ 15 billion with Kazakhstan and Uzbekistan respectively. About 2000 Chinese companies invested in 49 African countries. While visiting African Union in 2014, Chinese Premier Li Keqiang announced that China expects to achieve US $ 400 billion in trade volumes with Africa and raise its direct investment in the continent to US $ 100 billion by 2020. During the fourth China-Eurasia Expo of September 2015, about US $ 6 billion worth of foreign trade contracts were signed. China is not only eager in proposing several ambitious projects but is also backing up its projects with financial and economic arrangements like Silk Road Fund, China Development Bank, Shanghai Cooperation Organization and Asian Infrastructure and Investment Bank (AIIB), etc.

China's primary interests in Eurasian region are economic and trade related but, geostrategic element cannot be ruled out. There is gradual emergence of a politico-economic architecture driven by China as main contender that appears to be aiming to realize the twin objective of becoming leading economic power, and using this position as a counter to the US pivot to Asia. While India became a signatory to AIIB it is still not open to China's idea of OBOR, CPEC, etc. This paper attempts to study China's emerging position, its geopolitical initiatives in Eurasia in the previous decade, the long term geostrategic interests of China and imperatives for India in this context.

CHINA: THE EMERGING ECONOMY

China is the emerging economy of the world. While on nominal basis, China is the second largest country in the world in terms of GDP, it has overtaken USA in 2014 to become the largest on PPP basis. In terms of international merchandise trade in 2014, China ranks first followed closely by USA. A glance at Figure 1 shows the growth of the foreign trade of China over the past decade.

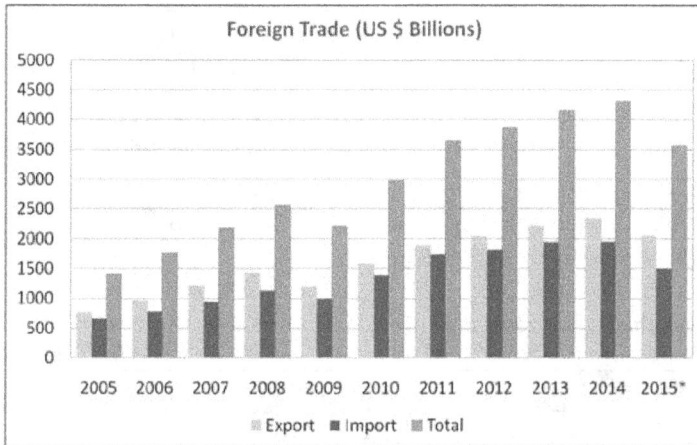

Fig. 1: Foreign Trade of China over the Past Decade

*Upto November 2015.

Source: National Bureau of Statistics, China.

Table 1 shows the trade of China with various countries from which it can be seen that China is emerging as a significant partner for many countries spanned over the extended region from East Europe, Central Asia and Eurasia and West Europe. It is entering into different sectors of economy by making agreements related to production, trade, assistance in development of infrastructure etc, in this region. Its exports span goods ranging from electronics, broadcasting equipment and telephones to small scale products like toys.

The new government in China under the leadership of Xi Jinping has announced two famous projects, the Silk Road Economic Belt (SREB) and the new Maritime Silk Route (MSR) in September and October 2013 respectively. Together they are known as One Belt, One Road (OBOR). Through SREB, the land based component of OBOR, China is expanding its relations with the countries situated along Central Asia, West Asia, Middle East and Europe. The main focus is on establishing connectivity and development of infrastructure like railroads, roads, ports and harbours. The proposed MSR extends from Quangzhou in Southeast China and traverses through South China Sea, the Indian Ocean, touching the eastern coast of Africa till it connects with Europe through Mediterranean. Thus, leveraging on this gigantic venture of OBOR, China is headed towards acquiring the strategic position at the global level, which is more or less now occupied by the US.

Table 1: Foreign Trade of China with various Regions in 2014

In US $ Billion

Region/ Country	Exports	Imports	Total	Remarks
USA	124	467	591	USA is the second largest trading partner with China
EU	215	356	571	China's biggest trading partner
Japan			340	Japan's largest trading partner
ASEAN	150	216	366	ASEAN is the biggest trading partner with China
Middle East			230	Grown 6 times in past decade
Africa	106	116	222	Africa is the biggest trading partner with China
Russia	53	42	95	Grown 6 times in past decade
India	60	12	72	For 2014–15. China is the largest trading partner for India
Central/East European			60	
Central Asia	24	21	45	

Source: Various online resources.

China is the 22nd complex economy according to the Economic Complexity Index (ECI)[1] as per the Observatory of the Economic Complexity conducted at the MIT Media lab. China's relations with the states in all terms—diplomatic, political and economic are also embarking new paths and becoming strong. With the fall of erstwhile Soviet Union and the end of the Cold War, the geopolitical dynamics in Eurasia witnessed a great shift, giving way to rapidly growing economies like China. Twenty first century is thus seen as wherein China is emerging as a leading economic power thus reminding one of Mackinder's theory of Heartland and end of the Columbian Epoch. Mackinder observed as long back as early 20th century that the future geopolitical dynamics are definitely ruled by land powers and the sea powers will take a back seat. The 'heartland' or 'pivot area' which was once under the Russian sphere of influence is now receiving close attention from China.

CHINA'S AGREEMENTS WITH EURASIAN COUNTRIES

With Russia

China has recently signed a number of deals with Russia in the areas of energy trade and finance, aimed to strengthening economic ties between the two countries. China's trade with Russia has been steadily increasing showing considerable growth in the recent years. In 2012, bilateral exchange reached US $ 87.5 billion. During his first official visit to Moscow in 2013, Chinese President Xi Jingping observed that the volume of bilateral exchange would be raised to 100 billion dollars in 2015 and 200 billion dollars in 2020.[2] China's investments in Russia have also been growing steadily over the past few years Chinese direct investment in Russia, including those via third countries totalled US $ 33 billion by 2014.[3]

This growth of China-Russia bilateral trade has paved way for rapid growth of two-way investment and comprehensive cooperation of China with Eurasian countries which in turn facilitated the construction of the SREB. To begin with, trade and economic policy matchmaking with Eurasian countries was promoted. The Ministry of Commerce (MOFCOM) of PRC proposed to found the China-Eurasia Economic Cooperation Fund; made active efforts to promote the signing of relevant agreements on strengthening the construction of the Silk Road Economic Belt under the framework of the bilateral trade and economic commission; signed the China-Kazakhstan medium and long term development plan; revised the management regulations of the China-Kazakhstan Khorgos Frontier International Cooperation Center agreed by the Chinese and Kazakhstan governments; and conducted feasibility studies on free trade agreements with relevant countries.

China also promoted exchange of high level visits to support the trade policy it has taken up with Eurasian countries. By 2015, MOFCOM was engaged in 37 high level exchange visits. It also signed 24 inter-governmental and inter-ministerial trade and economic agreements, and coordinated with enterprises and financial institutions to sign over 100 agreements with more than US$ 50 billion.[4]

When the Chinese Minister of Commerce Gao Hucheng visited Moscow and met the Eurasian Economic union's Trade Minister Andrey Slepnev, he said that China will enhance business ties with the bloc. This is clearly seen happening as China is a major trading partner with the member states of the union presently. Zhoud Shijian, the Standing Councillor at China Society for World Trade Organisation Studies, said the consensus is a strategic decision with a long term perspective.[5]

During the summit meeting of Putin and Xi Jingping on May 8, 2015, the two leaders signed a joint declaration on 'cooperation in coordinating development of EEU and the Silk Road Economic Belt'. China will also invest US $ 5.8 billion in the construction of the Moscow-Kazan High Speed Railway.[6]

Moscow and Beijing declared a goal to coordinate the two projects in order to build a "common economic space" in Eurasia, including a Free Trade Agreement between the EEU and China. China has not only recognised the EEU which came into existence on 1 January 2015, but also expressed its willingness to deal with the union collectively and not only engage with the individual member states separately. Such moves clearly show the eagerness of China in making its own position strong in the Central Asia. It has already become a major investor in Central Asia. While the FTA between EEU and China is yet to happen, meanwhile, Russia is said to be looking for the Chinese infrastructure investment and secure access to the US $ 40 billion "Silk Road Fund" for upgrading Russia's infrastructure.

Connectivity is the key aspect of the proposed OBOR projects. China's MOFCOM has been working actively to engage Russia's trans-Siberian Railway with the SREB, and made positive progress in the construction of the China-Russia Tongjiang-Nizhneleninskoye railway bridge and the Heihe highway bridge. The first phase of China-Tajikistan Highway was completed.

Recently, China and the Eurasian Economic Union (EAEU) had signed an agreement on information exchange between customs services of China and the Union countries. During the third round of negotiations supervised by Member of Board- Minister in Charge of Customs Cooperation of the EEC, Vladimir Goshin, which took place in Irkutsk from 25–27 August 2015, this agreement was completed.[7]

Vladimir Goshin, elaborating on this agreement said that its purpose was the exchange of information about goods which are in transit from the People's Republic of China through the Eurasian Economic Union Member states or from the EAEU and transported through China to third countries. Such exchanges of information will increase the level of trust between the member states of EAEU and the PRC.

In September 2015, Russia and China signed an agreement on Belkomur railroad involving financing and construction of

712 kilometers of new railroad and modernization of 449 kilometers of railroad that already exists.

With Kazakhstan

In March 2015, China entered into an agreement with Kazakhstan worth US $ 23.6 billion to help restructure the Central Asian country's economy. In August 2015, China signed an agreement with Kazakhstan of US $ 600 million to develop a special trade and economic zone in KTZE— Khorgos Gateway on Kazakhstan's eastern border with China which is expected to be completed in 2018. After completion, this zone will function as one of the largest international transport logistics and distribution centres. This will also provide Kazakhstan, China and other countries of the Eurasian region with new opportunities for the access to the world markets. East Kazakhstan also signed seven business agreements worth $ 1.7 billion, in mid-November 2015.

With Kyrgyzstan

China signed an agreement on 17 December 2015 for design and construction of the cross-border section of the Russia-China natural gas pipeline. The entire pipeline is slated to be completed by the end of 2018. The Chinese National Petroleum Corporation (CNPC) also announced an agreement on December 16 for construction of the 134-mile Kyrgyzstan section of Line D of the Central Asia-China gas pipeline.

With Belarus

In May 2015, China signed a number of agreements with Belarus. They include Chinese investment in Belarusian railroads, industrial enterprises, and Big Stone—a Belarusian-Chinese industrial park. China also suggested that Belarus would participate in the proposed New Silk Road.

With Armenia

In March 2015, China signed a bilateral comprehensive declaration with Armenia. One of the document's significant pillars is Armenia's enrolment in China's "Silk Road Economic Belt". Another is an accord to cooperate in the defence and military sphere, emphasizing mutual military support. The declaration combined over ten special agreements, involving various ministries of both states, and a preferential loan for adapting and modernizing custom services.

With other Eurasian Countries

Apart from signing various agreements with the member countries of the EEU, China has also been expanding its relations with other Eurasian countries. Uzbekistan and China signed agreements in September 2013 worth US $ 15 billion in key sectors, including the exploitation of oil, gas and uranium fields. Under the Framework of "Silk Road Economic Belt" Initiative was signed between China and Uzbekistan in June 2015.

In May 2014, Turkmenistan and China signed the Treaty of Friendship and Cooperation; a joint declaration on the development and deepening of the strategic Partnership and the statement on the acceptance of the Plan for development of the strategic partnership between the two countries for 2014–2018.

By 2015, China signed twenty four inter-governmental and inter-ministerial trade and economic agreements with Eurasian countries and coordinated with enterprises and financial institutions to sign over hundred agreements with more than US $ 50 billion.

In Aug 2015, China and the EEU also signed an agreement on information exchange between customs services of China and the Union countries and an agreement on Expanding

Mutually Beneficial Trade and Economic Cooperation. In September 2015, leaders of the 5 member states signed documents making China an official partner to the trading bloc of EEU.

GEOSTRATEGIC INTERESTS OF CHINA IN EURASIA

Collapse of Soviet Union and the emergence of newly independent states in Central Asia in close proximity to China, exposed a new fluid geopolitical scenario on its western border. The region became a hotbed of competing external forces. Subsequent outbreak of civil war in bordering Tajikistan and instability in neighbouring Afghanistan, the security situation in central Asia became a constant factor weighing on Chinese policy makers.

While the decline of Russian influence in Central Asia paved way for China's interests in the region and Eurasia, it can also be seen as a response to the 'pivot' or 'rebalance' of US to Asia. Domestically, Beijing had to focus on the intensifying opposition of Uighur and Tibetan opposition against Chinese rule since 2007–08 upraises. Since these two are in the Eurasian frontier region, a hold on them became imperative for China and hence the need to work on economic development and modernisation of these areas. The OBOR, particularly the SREB component is thus driven by both grand regional and domestic imperatives of Beijing's Eurasian policy.

China began focusing on Xinjiang Uighur Autonomous Region (XUAR) and other western provinces after 2000, through the "western development" programme. In 2012 Wang Jisi, Dean of the School of articulated the idea of Marching Westwards as a rebalancing act of China's geo-strategy. As the United States has pivoted towards the Asia-Pacific, Wang urged Chinese policy makers not to limit their interests to the Asia-Pacific, but rather to develop a plan to advance relations with China's western-frontier neighbours, including Central Asia, South Asia, and the Middle East and furthermore, to form a Eurasian cooperation framework from London to Shanghai. This idea would not only facilitate economic and cultural relations with the countries to the west of China, but also domestically, "it would accelerate the 'Grand Western Development', a national strategy launched in 2000, to promote the growth of China's western provinces, in light of its unbalanced development compared to the eastern coastal provinces". SREB forms a key component of China's Eurasian pivot, and Central Asia is assuming a new strategic importance in China's overall foreign policy. In contrast to Western Europe or East Asia, the Central Asian region is 'free from a US-dominated regional order or a pre-existing economic integration mechanism".

There are compelling geopolitical reasons, such as energy security, for China to push forward with its one belt one road plans at a time when its trading partners are potentially excluding it from strategic agreements. Trans-pacific partnerships, the transatlantic trade and investment partnership and the EU-Japan agreement show comprehensive liberalisation agendas, but do not include China and have the potential to increase trading costs. In response China plans to negotiate free-trade agreements with 65 countries along the OBOR.

China knows well that its development is linked to Asia and beyond, and in part, is banking its future on responding to its neighbours' huge infrastructure needs via One Belt, One Road. Meanwhile China's growing domestic market means the chance for the region and the world to capitalise by providing goods and services.

In order to meet a growing need for raw materials, access to Central Asia's raw materials particularly, oil and gas, and potentially use its transit capabilities was felt essential by

China. Further, China's top priority is to stimulate the domestic economy via exports from industries with major over capacity such as steel, cement, and aluminium. China has low internal consumption. China's leadership is looking for new channels to sustain its appetite for growth at a time when developing neighbours are experiencing rapidly rising demand. These imperatives made China look towards West.

As a part of the OBOR, on land, the initiative will focus on jointly building a new Eurasian Land Bridge and developing China-Mongolia-Russia, China-Central Asia-West Asia and China-Indochina Peninsula economic corridors.

Though China has not joined the Eurasian Union it has been making investments in Central Asia, especially energy, which can secure its interests. Since stability of any region is supported by arrangements like the EEU, which is an essential input for economic collaboration, Beijing is positively for such union.

China ranked first in its imports to Kazakhstan, Kyrgyzstan and first in its exports in Tajkistan, Turkemistan. In terms of total trade, China ranks first with Kyrgyzstan and second in Kazakhstan, Tajkistan, Turkenistan and Uzbekistan. Thus it can be seen that these five Central Asian countries and China are significant economic partners of each other. Kazakhstan and Turkmenistan are vital countries for China due to their possession of huge Hydrocarbon reserves. In order to sustain its growth China needs the continuous flow of these resources to itself. Thus, Kazakhstan-China Oil Pipeline and the Central Asia Natural Gas Pipeline Projects can be regarded as good examples of the Partnership between Beijing, Astana and Ashgabat.

According to estimates given by the Chinese government, China's trade with Eurasian countries in 2013 reached US $ 1.25 trillion and is estimated to double by 2020.[8]

China has become an official partner to the trading bloc of EEU, when leaders of the five member states signed documents to that effect, in early September 2015 in Borovoe in Kazakhstan. The union has signed documents making Israel and China official partners, and also signed on another agreement authorising the creation of a free trade zone.[9] Due to this agreement all Chinese goods that are headed towards Europe through Kazakhstan will now pass through without paying tax. While this is an added facility to China, it could weaken the economy of Kazakhstan.

IMPERATIVES FOR INDIA

There is more to the Belt and Road initiative than meets the eye. It is not just a network of rail and road links, and connecting ports through sea routes. It is more about enhancing policy coordination, trade liberalisation, financial integration and connectivity including people to people links, across Asia, Africa and Europe, i.e., integrating development strategies of countries along the Belt and Road. It certainly is a grand geostrategic initiative of the 21st century.

Of all the regions, the European occupies a significant position as it becomes a vital link for China in securing influence on eastern and western ends of Eurasia. Carefully selected nodal points along the land corridor and terminal points along the maritime corridor are a clear indication of this aspect. For instance, Hungary is chosen as a key logistics hub on the trans-Siberian Link. It may serve as a distribution point for Chinese exports to Europe and an aggregating point for imports from Europe.[10]

As an immediate neighbour, and as a rapidly growing economy which is expected to be catching up with the rest of the leading economies, India is now closely watching the multifarious activities and projects that are being taken up by China under the OBOR initiative. India's foreign policy and its relations with the rest of the world have undergone significant changes in the Post-Cold war period. With the launch of Look East Policy India's relations have tremendously developed particularly with Southeast Asia and beyond, extending up to Asia Pacific. However, in the light of the newly proposed—and financially heavily backed up—ambitious initiatives of the OBOR gaining momentum, it becomes imperative that India should reconsider its own position in the region and response to the emerging geostrategic environment. As it is, many countries in Asia, Europe and South America are responding to China's OBOR call. About 40 government officials, scholars and researchers from these countries attended the SREB Cities International Forum, held in Yiwu of Zhegiang province in China in August 2015. The theme of this forum was 'Unimpeded Trade, Co-build prosperity'.

Under the OBOR initiative, China is developing ports in Bangladesh, Sri Lanka and Pakistan which builds up the Chinese commercial and military facilities and relationships in the Indian Ocean. CPEC corridor, which is an integral part of SREB, connects Kashgar to Gwadar besides running through the strategic Gilgit-Baltistan region of POK and hence may have a bearing of China's influence on the India-Pak border disputes in the area. CPEC is particularly significant for India since Gwadar port is one of the points where the Road and the Belt intersect each other. India is uncertain whether the OBOR initiative is merely economic or has security orientations.

China is making huge investments in India's immediate neighbourhood. This may come under the China's sphere of influence which could be a setback to India. With the development of an alternative to the traditional maritime routes, India's growing influence as emerging maritime power will come under challenge in the Indian Ocean and South China Sea regions.

CONCLUSION AND RECOMMENDATIONS

The logical step for India would be to stand up to the competition and develop alternative connectivity networks on a global scale. However, presently India does not possess either the political or economic strength to take on such a crucial task. Moreover, the potential that is required to reach the status of a resourceful trade partner, a supportive market for finished products, and a reliable source of financial assistance involves time. China on the other hand, is already proving itself in all these areas. The OBOR route passes in close vicinity to India. Hence it would be prudent for India to leverage on the infrastructure being built with the initiative of China while working on alternative networks. To address its security concerns, India can consider seeking modifications to the CPEC corridor. India can utilise the OBOR for promoting its own 'Make in India' initiative.

OBOR is more or less projected as an economic and development initiative mainly focused on connectivity. But observers in the rest of the world see it also as about security and energy, entailing a higher level of Chinese military presence in the South China Sea, the Indian Ocean, the Persian Gulf and the Mediterranean, (for *e.g.*, the new military base in Djibouti). India should therefore initiate dialogue and discussions on security architecture, such as Track I and Track II with China.

Though China is making huge inroads in India's neighbourhood through trade and investments, India is perceived with better credibility. In this context, India needs to—leverage on its credibility; focus on immediate neighbourhood in political, economic and cultural relationships; and consider active co-operation in its neighbourhood to assist in their development. The 'Neighbourhood-First' concept being pursued by the present Government needs to be given a definite shape and taken further into an active collaboration.

India should also work towards stability in the region to enhance trade facilities and secure economic interests eventually in Central Asia and the Middle East. It needs to explore its own option in the lines of TPP in Asia-Pacific and the Transatlantic Trade and Investment Partnership (TTIP).

India has to develop its own connectivity and particularly focus on building Indian Ocean network of ports, with connecting highways and rail routes such as the Mekong—Ganga corridor, Sittwe-Mizoram multi-modal transport corridor. India also needs to expedite developing the deep water port on Sri Lanka's eastern coast Trincomalee, as a major energy and transport hub. There have been long standing plans but the progress has been very slow and disappointing. The Lanka branch of IOC has taken over one million ton capacity at a World War II vintage Oil Tank Farm at Trincomalee on a 35 year lease and has also acquired 100 gas stations all over Sri Lanka in 2003 but not much is happening since the Indian Oil acquired the tank farm more than a decade ago.

Andaman and Nicobar Islands are very important to India. These territorial Islands of India lie at the very centre of Bay of Bengal and could be developed to serve as a regional shipping hub for the littoral states and beyond. However, India does not appear to recognise their geostrategic significance beyond using them as distant outpost. The potential of Andaman and Nicobar Islands can be developed to serve as a regional shipping hub for the littoral states and beyond.

India is now required to 'Look West' too. It can plan and build infrastructural components such as rail and road links to connect Central Asia through West Asian countries. For example the port of Chahbahar in Iran could be used as a main link and get to use the Chinese built routes to access both Central Asian and Russian destinations as well as Europe.

India should develop its own strategy regarding CPEC and BCIM corridors. Both are independent initiatives, but closely related to the larger idea of OBOR. Interestingly, CPEC and BCIM do not intersect either, and only touch India's periphery, without linking South and Central Asia. India stands virtually in the pivotal position of the geographical area encircled by OBOR and not gaining much from it as of now. Thus India must identify those elements of the OBOR on which there is congruence of interests or mutuality of benefits between itself and China.

REFERENCES

[1] Economic Complexity Rankings (2013). http://atlas.media. mit.edu/en/rankings/country. Accessed on 04 November, 2015.

[2] Huaxia-ed., English.news.cn., "China, Russia to increase Bilateral investment, financial cooperation". 18 June 2015. http://news. xinhuanet.com/english/2015-06/18/c_134335445.htm. Accessed on 03 December 2015.

[3] Ministry of Commerce-People's Republic of China, http:// english.mofcom.gov.cn/sys/print.shtml?/zt_businessreview/news/ 201503/20150300908061. Accessed 10 December.

[4] Nan, Zhong, "China vows to enhance trade with Eurasian bloc". *China Daily*, 11 May 2015. http://www.chinadaily.com.cn/ world/cn_eu/2015-05/11/content_20676192.htm. Accessed on 10 December 2015.

[5] Sidorenko, Tatiana, "The Scope of Economic Cooperation between Russia and China and Future Prospects". *Universidad Nacional*. Vol. 45, No. 176, January–March 2014, http:// www.probdes.iiec.unam.mx/en/revistas/v45n176/body/v45n176 a2_1.php. Accessed on 26 November 2015.

[6] More, R.T. Question, "Russia, China agree to integrate Eurasian Union, Silk Road, sign deals". 08 May 2015. https://www. rt.com/business/256877-russia-china-deals-cooperation. Accessed on 05 December 2015.

[7] EEC: Eurasian Economic Commission-News and Events, 'The EAEU and China have reached new agreements in the field of information exchange between the customs services of China and Union countries'. 28 August 2015. http://www.eurasiancommiss ion.org/en/nae/news/Pages/28-08-2015-1.aspx. Accessed on 10 December 2015.

[8] Esteban, Mario and Otero-Iglesias, Miguel. "What are the prospects for the new Chinese-led Silk Road and Asian Infrastructure Investment Bank?" Royal Institute, ELCANO. 17 April 2015. http://www.realinstitutoelcano.org/wps/portal/web/rielcano_en/ contenido?WCM_GLOBAL_CONTEXT=/elcano/elcano_in/zo nas_in/ari23-2015-esteban-oteroiglesias-what-are-prospects-for-new-chinese-led-silk-road-and-asian-infrastructure-investment-bank. Accessed on 05 December 2015.

[9] Kseniya Bondal, "Eurasian Economic Union Closes Deal with Israel, China", *SILK ROADREPORTERS,* 17 November 2015. http://www. silkroadreporters.com/2015/11/17/eurasian-econo mic-union-closes-deal-with-israel-china. Accessed on 12 Dec. 2015.

[10] Saran, Shyam, "What China's One Belt and One Road Strategy Means for India, Asia and the World". *The Wire.* 09 October, 2015, http://thewire.in/2015/10/09/what-chinas-one-belt-and-one-road-strategy-means-for-india-asia-and-the-world-12532. Accessed on 14 December 2015.

BIBILIOGRAPHY

1. Aneja, Atul, "One belt One road' Initiative". *Frontline,* 01 May 2015. http://www.frontline.in/world-affairs/one-belt-one-road-initiative/article 7098506.ece. Accessed on 14 December 2015.

2. Bondal, Kseniya, "Eurasian Economic Union Closes Deal with Israel, China". *SILK ROAD REPORTERS,* 17 November 2015. http://www.silkroadreporters.com/2015/11/17/eurasian-economic-union-closes-deal-with-israel-china. Accessed on 12 December 2015.

3. Borroz, Nicholas and Marston, Hunter, "Asia's Infrastructure Investment Battle". *Diplomat,* 11 June 2015. http://thediplomat. com/2015/06/ asias-infrastructure-investment-battle. Accessed on 14 December 2015.

4. Briefing, China, "China Insitutionalises Eurasia for Silk Road Development". 23 June 2015. http://www.china-briefing. com/news/2015/06/ 23/china-institutionalizes-eurasia-silk-road-development.html. Accessed on 11 December 2015.

5. Briefing, China, "Stability and Development-Twin Concerns for China in Central Asia". 17 August 2010.http://www.china-briefing.com/news/ 2010/08/17/stability-and-development-twin-concerns-for-china-in-central-asia.html. Accessed on 17 Dec. 2015.

6. Briefing, China, "The New Eurasian Economic Union—A China FTA in the Offing?". 09 January 2015. http://www.china-briefing.com/news/2015/01/09/new-eurasian-economic-union—china-fta-offing.html. Accessed on 10 December 2015.

7. Clarke, Michael, "Understanding China's Eurasian Pivot". *Diplomat*, 10 September 2015. http://thediplomat.com/2015/ 09/understanding-chinas-eurasian-pivot. Accessed on 30 November 2015.

8. Dawber, Alistair, "China to Spain cargo train: Successful first 16, 156-mile round trip on world's longest railway brings promise of increased trade". *INDEPENDENT*, 24 February 2015. http:// www.independent.co.uk/news/world/europe/china-to-spain-cargo-train-successful-first-16156-mile-round-trip-on-worlds-longest-brings-10067895.html. Accessed on 14 December 2015.

9. Economic Complexity Rankings (2013). http://atlas.media.mit. edu/en/rankings/country. Accessed on 04 November 2015.

10. EEC News and Events, "EAEU and China have reached new agreements in the field of information and exchange between the customs services of China and Union countries. 28 August 2015. http://www.eurasian commission.org/en/nae/news/Pages/28-08-2015-1.aspx. Accessed on 10 December 2015.

11. Esteban, Mario and Otero-Iglesias, Miguel, "What are the prospects for the new Chinese-led Silk Road and Asian Infrastructure Investment Bank?", Royal Institute, ELCANO, 17 April 2015. http://www.realinstitu toelcano.org/wps/portal/web/rielcano_en/ contenido?WCM_GLOBAL_CONTEXT=/elcano/elcano_in/zo nas_in /ari23-2015-esteban-oteroiglesias-what-are-prospects-for-new-chinese-led-silk-road-and-asian-infrastructure-investment-bank. Accessed on 05 December 2015.

12. Gabuev, Alexander, "Eurasian Silk Road Union: Towards a Russia-China Consensus?" *Diplomat*, 05 June 2015. http://the

diplomat.com/2015/06/eurasian-silk-road-union-towards-a-russia-china-consensus. Accessed on 06 December 2015.

13. Hartwell, Christopher, "China is the key to the future of the Eurasian Economic Union". *Russia Direct*, 12 February 2015. http://www.russia-direct.org/opinion/china-key-future-eurasian-economic-union. Accessed on 13 December 2015.

14. HKTDC Research, "An Overview of Central Asian Markets on the Silk Road Economic Belt". 19 November 2015. http://hkmb. hktdc.com/en/1X0A4C4W/hktdc-research/An-Overview-of-Cent ral-Asian-Markets-on-the-Silk-Road-Economic-Belt. Accessed on 08 December 2015.

15. Huaxia, Ed., English.news.cn. China, Russia to increase bilateral Investment, financial cooperation". 18 June 2015. http://news. xinhuanet.com/english/2015-06/18/c_134335445.htm. Accessed on 03 December 2015.

16. "India, EEU to Benefit from Silk Road Economic Corridor". *Financial Tribune*, 02 September 2015. http://financialtribune. com/articles/world-economy/24866/ india-eeu-benefit-silk-road-economic-corridor. Accessed on 08 December 2015.

17. Kennedy, Trevor and Yin, David, "The Future of Free Trade in Asia-Pacific: China's Eurasian Dilemma". *Forbes*, 24 November 2015. http://www.forbes.com/sites/davidyin/2015/11/24/the-future-of-free-trade-in-asia-pacific-chinas-eurasian-dilemma/#408 735a3a286. Accessed on 09 December 2015.

18. Kikuchi, Tomoo and Masutomo, Takehiro, NUS, "China infrastructure gambit in Southeast Asia". *EASTASIAFORUM*, 15 May 2015. http://www.Eastasiaforum.org/2015/05/15/chinas-infrastructure-gambit-in-southeast-asia.
Accessed on 15 Dec. 2015.

19. Kisacik, Sina, "China's Approach toward the Eurasian Economic Union". *HAZAR-*Strateji Enstitusu. 28 February 2014. http://www.hazar.org/blogdetail/blog/china%E2%80%99s_appr oach_toward_the_eurasian_economic_union_918.aspx. Accessed on 11 December 2015.

20. Liu, Zhen and wu, Wendy, "China puts links with central and eastern Europe on the fast track". *South China Morning Post*, 25 November 2015. http://www.scmp.com/news/china/diplomacy-defence/article/1883411/china-puts-links-central-and-eastern-eur-ope-fast-track. Accessed on 13 December 2015.

21. Lukin, Artyom, "Mackinder Revisited: Will China Establish Eurasian Empire 3.0?", *Diplomat*, 07 February 2015. http://thediplomat.com/2015/02/mackinder-revisited-will-china-establish-eurasian-empire-3-0. Accessed on 26 October 2015.

22. Marantidou, Virginia and Cossa, Ralph A., "China and Russia's Great Game in Central Asia". *National Interest*, 01 October 2014. http://nationalinterest.org/blog/the-buzz/china-russias-great-game-central-asia-11385. Accessed on 05 December 2015.

23. Nan, Zhong, "China vows to enhance trade with Eurasian bloc". *Chinadaily*, 11 May 2015. http://www.chinadaily.com.cn/world/cn_eu/2015-05/11/content_20676192.htm. Accessed on 10 December 2015.

24. More, R.T. Question, "Russia China Agree to Integrate Eurasian Union, Silk Road, Silk Road". 08 May 2015. https://www.rt.com/business/256877-russia-china-deals-cooperation. Accessed on 05 December 2015.

25. Saran, Shyam, "What China's One Belt and One Road Strategy Means for India, Asia and the World". *WIRE*, 09 October 2015. http://thewire.in/2015/10/09/what-chinas-one-belt-and-one-road-strategy-means-for-india-asia-and-the-world-12532. Accessed on 14 December 2015.

26. Sidorenko, Tatiana, "The Scope of Economic Cooperation between Russia and China and Future Prospects". *Universidad Nacional*. Vol. 45, No. 176, January–March 2014 http://www.probdes.iiec.unam.mx/en/revistas/v45n176/body/v45n176a2_1.php. Accessed on 26 November 2015.

27. Skulska, Boguslawa Drelich; Bobowski, Sebastian; Jankowiak, Anna H. and Skulski, Przemyslaw, "China's Trade Policy Towards Central and Eastern Europe in the 21st Century, Example of Poland". De Gruyter, /*Folia Oeconomica Stetinensia*, DOI: 10.2478/foli-2014-0111. http://www.degruyter.com/view/j/foli.2014.14.issue-1/foli-2014-0111/foli-2014-0111. xml. Accessed on 13 December 2015.

28. Standish, Reid, "China Russia Lay Foundation for Massive Economic Cooperation". *FP Passport*, 10 July 2015. http://foreignpolicy.com/2015/07/10/china-russia-sco-ufa-summit-putin-xi-jinping-eurasian-union-silk-road. Accessed on 10 December 2015.

29. Tao, Xie, "Is This China's Eurasian Century? China's response to the U.S. Pivot to Asia—A 'march west'—faces serious hurdles".

Diplomat, 10 October 2015. http://thediplomat.com/2015/10/
is-this-chinas-eurasian-century/. Accessed on 31 October 2015.

30. Tiezzi, Shannon, "China's 'Belt and Road' Reaches Europe".
    Diplomat, 26 November 2015. http://thediplomat.com/2015/11/
    chinas-belt-and-road-reaches-europe. Accessed on 03 December
    2015.

31. "The One Belt, One Road Initiatives-1". Maritime Insight Issue
    1, June 2015. http://www.icms.polyu.edu.hk/research_maritime
    Insight/2015-Jun-en/3.pdf. Accessed on 14 December 2015.

32. Tukmadiyeva, Malika, "Xinjiang in China's Foreign Policy
    toward Central Asia". *Connections*-Quarterly Journal, 12 March
    2005. http://connections-qj.org/article/xinjiang-chinas-foreign-
    policy-toward-central-asia. Accessed on 10 December 2015.

33. Vikkokst'maus, "China surpasses Russia as top trading partner
    for Central Asian countries". *BOFIT Weekly*, 2013/39. 27
    September 2013. http://www.suomenpankki.fi/bofit_en/seuran
    ta/seuranta-aineisto/pages/vw20133 9_5. aspx. Accessed on 12
    December 2015.

34. Webster, Graham, "How China Maintains Strategic Ambiguity
    in the South China Sea". *Diplomat*, 29 October 2015.
    http://thediplomat.com/2015/10/how-china-maintains-strategic-
    ambiguity-in-the-south-china-sea. Accessed on 01 November
    2015.

35. Xinhua, "China, CEE countries to accelerate win-win cooperation".
    Chinadaily, 24 November 2015. http://www.chinadaily.com.cn/
    world/2015liattendsASEAN/2015-11/24/content_22515493.
    htm. Accessed on 13 December 2015.

The Emergence of New Institutions for Development Cooperation and the Impact on India China Relations

Sukalpa Chakrabarti

The economic reforms of the 90s in the developing countries were poised to bring about a transformation in the global market system. However the post reform era revealed an austere growth trajectory for the countries. The Latin American crises, not just put a halt to the reform era but what ensued was years of lost growth opportunity. The starkest scenario was in Sub-Saharan Africa which was enmeshed in extreme poverty and debt. The Middle East which had countries reeling under stagnation became the breeding ground for terror activities. Finally the currency crisis dealt a major blow to the promising growth take off exhibited by the Asian Tigers.

However the steady growth of both China and India, post the adoption of liberation strategies, came to the rescue. It had ripple effects on the world market due to increased demand for raw materials to fuel its export-led growth. This acted as a boost to the African and Latin American economies, as commodity prices ascended. With the developing economies recovering from their downturn, BRICS[1] began to emerge as a major powerhouse. BRICS have created the Contingency Reserve Arrangements (CRA) in BRICS countries to provide official liquidity when balance of payments adjustments are needed. Additionally, China is also backing the Asian Infrastructure Investment Bank (AIIB) with 57 potential member countries, including all major European economies (such as Germany, the United Kingdom and France), alongside the creation of the New Silk Road fund to invest in infrastructure connections within Asia as well as those linking to Europe and Africa. The setting up of the New Development Bank (NDB) dedicated to the emerging BRICS countries, in China's commercial hub of Shanghai, is seen by many as a counter to the International Monetary Fund and the World Bank.

BRICS AND THE ECONOMIC ORDER

With a shift in the global economic balance of power towards Asia, the failure of the Washington Consensus and the Bretton Woods twins in spite of conditionalities, structural adjustment programmes and "reforms", financial meltdown and the collapse of leading banks and financial institutions in the West, there had been an urgent need for new thinking and new instruments for the building of a new economic order. Existing global economic governance organizations such as the IMF, WTO, and World Bank are all hampered by redundant processes and low proficiency. A critical flaw in the present structure of global economic governance is that of under representation of developing countries in international economic organizations. The present structure and the rules of governance were designed primarily by the developed countries over the past fifty years; and these are no longer a perfect fit to the challenges and opportunities apparent in the steady growth of the developing countries and emerging economies. The resolution of global issues of significance is impossible without the active involvement of these emerging giants. There is no denying that the present global economic order is reflective of a meritocracy. The BRICS countries are seriously underrepresented given the inflexible vote share. e.g. China has only a four percent voting share in the IMF, even though it accounts for more than sixteen percent of global GDP and over 19 percent of world population.[2] The obvious solution suggested by the supporters of the current system is that the BRICS could increase their voting shares by contributing more to the two institutions; but what is conveniently ignored is that the prerogative of sole veto power for the United States limits the utility of such investment.

Consequently, the BRICS have adopted the route of the New Development Bank to exert their strength. In a unique move to combine the functions of both the World Bank and the IMF in one, the NDB is slated to provide both development grants and emergency reserves. The NDB will begin with a US $ 50 billion capital divided equally between its five founders, with an initial total of $ 10 billion put in cash over the next seven years and $ 40 billion in guarantees. BRICS have also created the Contingency Reserve Arrangements (CRA) to provide official liquidity—a US $ 100 billion currency exchange reserve—which members can tap in case of balance of payment crises. China, the biggest foreign exchange reserve-holder amongst them, will contribute the major portion of the currency pool. Brazil, India and Russia will contribute $ 18 billion each while South Africa will chip in with $ 5 billion. During crisis, China will be eligible to ask for half its contribution, South Africa for double its contribution while the others can receive back what they put in.[3]

To do away with non-egalitarian voting rights, the five founding members have been given to hold a minimum of 55 percent voting power between them at all times (of which they will hold equal shares); while the future members are to split the remaining 45 percent equally. As the global economy is being churned, it is but natural that new models and approaches towards more inclusive and equitable developmental goals are being explored. In the process, the developing block has set out by focusing on the complementarities and building on their respective strengths.

New attempts to multilateralize flows of assistance are likely to contribute significantly to global development and defend the virtues of competitive pluralism and further promote global consensus in development cooperation around the normative and instrumental value of accountability, transparency, participation and inclusion.

BRICS DEVELOPMENT BANK AND SOUTH-SOUTH COOPERATION

Research in the field shows that some emerging and developing economies have accumulated very large long-term foreign exchange assets, and their share in the world total, as well as the absolute level of foreign exchange reserves accumulated, has also grown remarkably in the last decade. Predictably, a huge chunk of these resources are invested in developed countries, with relatively low yields. Parallely, there exists critical but unmet needs in the emerging and developing countries, in the fields of infrastructure and sustainable development. A study by Bhattacharya, Romani and Stern, 2012; Bhattacharya and Romani, 2013[4] identified a deficit of investment of up to around US $ 1 trillion annually. Should this huge deficit remain unaddressed then it would result in constraining future growth of the developing and emerging economies. The fact that emerging and developing countries have the necessary savings and foreign exchange reserves to finance a new development bank that could contribute to finance such investment makes a clear case for such an institution to be created.[5] Not only would it help to reinforce the voice of developing and emerging economies in the development finance architecture, but it will also provide the much needed funding of long-term investments in infrastructure and sustainable development.

I. Most regional and multilateral development banks have commenced operations with a major focus on infrastructure—

be it the World Bank or the European Investment Bank. The same holds true for the BRICS development bank, which is also aiming for enhanced investment in infrastructure and more sustainable development, based on the need for growth, structural change, inclusion as well as sustainability and resilience.

It is a given that lack of infrastructure is a barrier to growth. Therefore the developing countries need increase in infrastructure investment to quicken economic growth and development and reduce the existent levels of inequality. As countries move from primary to secondary and tertiary sector-based economies, infrastructure needs expanding. With projections of about two billion people moving into urban centres in emerging and developing countries in the next three decades, there is no denying the emergent need for major investments in urban infrastructure. Infrastructure is also crucial for increasing access to basic services by poor people. With stark figures staring the world in the face—such as 1.4 billion people having no access to electricity, 0.9 billion people having no access to clean drinking water and 2.6 billion lacking access to sanitation—the disparity can no longer be ignored. Parallely, environmental sustainability requires new infrastructural support. This would call for reduction in the environmental impacts of prevailing infrastructure and coming up with new designs that would promote environmentally sustainable lifestyles.

To meet these objectives, Bhattacharya, Romani and Stern[6] have estimated the annual need for infrastructure investment. They project broadly that investment spending in infrastructure (excluding operation and maintenance) in emerging and developing countries will need to increase from approximately US $ 0.8–0.9 trillion per year currently, to approximately US $ 1.8–2.3 trillion per year by 2020, or from around three per cent of GDP to 6–8 per cent of emerging and developing countries' GDP. This includes about US $

200–300 billion to ensure that infrastructure results in lower emissions and is more resilient to climate change.

The main source of financing investment in infrastructure at present are national government budgets, which fund well over 50 per cent of the total; this national public share rises further if investment by national development banks is added, with the total of both categories summing up to US $ 570–650 billion annually. The other source is private finance, which is estimated to provide US $ 150–250 billion annually. One problem of this type of funding is that it is very pro-cyclical, and tends to fall during and after crises; the 1997–1998 East Asian crisis being a case in point. Private finance is also heavily concentrated in certain sectors, such as tele-communications, and in middle-income countries. Overseas Development Aid and existing Multilateral Development Banks (MDBs) finance provide only an estimated US $ 40–60 billion annually, and South-South flows are estimated to finance only around US $ 20 billion or less annually.[7]

The decision to focus the operations of the NDB on this area stands validated by the fact that the unmet needs in the area of infrastructure and sustainable development are extremely large and that such investment is crucial for inclusive and more sustainable growth—with only half of it currently being met by existing financial sources. It is important for the move towards a greener economy that investment in infrastructure is broadly defined, so it also includes infrastructure investment such as for renewable energy, like solar, wind and others. The NDB's objective can come to encompass financing innovation for both the development of such technologies and their adaptation to the conditions of emerging and developing economies.

II. In the context of the role of the New Development Bank in South-South Cooperation, apart from addressing the need of development finance, another critical requirement is the need for the provision of short-term liquidity. This is needed to create a buffer to the potential vulnerability of the emerging and developing economies to external shocks coming from the developed economies. The short-term balance of payments financing provided by the IMF is often insufficient, and more significantly tied to inappropriate conditionality. The NDB can step in to bridge the gap, building on the experience of and complementing existing institutions. The BRICS Contingent Reserve Arrangement (CRA), as discussed earlier, is a self-managed stabilization fund of US $ 100 billion in reserves, set up to provide mutual liquidity in the event of a balance of payment crisis. This would certainly have a positive precautionary effect and further strengthen global financial stability.

Examples of other South-South financial collaboration include the original Chang Mai Initiative—which has evolved into the 10+3 foreign-exchange reserves pool established by the Association of South-East Asian Nations (ASEAN) plus China, Japan, and the Republic of Korea, with a size of 240 billion US dollars, called CMIM, or Chang Mai Initiative Multilateralization—and the smaller-scale Fondo Latino Americano de Reserve (FLAR).The CMIM also shares a similar objective of reinforcing the capacity of its member states to shield themselves against augmented risks and challenges in the global economy. The core objectives are to address balance-of-payments and short-term liquidity difficulties in the region, as well as to supplement existing international financial arrangements. CMIM is limited to a regional grouping and to a currency swap. Moreover, it remains linked to the IMF, as only 30 per cent of a member's quota is accessible without the prior agreement of an IMF programme.[8] Thus, one likely key difference from the CMIM is that the BRICS CRA will not include a link to the IMF, which brings about policy conditionality in the event of crisis[9] In this sense the BRICS CRA would be similar to the FLAR, which has no link with IMF conditionality.

NDB AND AIIB

Additionally, China is also backing the Asian Infrastructure Investment Bank (AIIB) with 57 potential member countries, including all major European economies (such as Germany, the United Kingdom and France), alongside the creation of the New Silk Road Bank to fund investment in infrastructure connections within Asia as well as those linking to Europe and Africa.

The NDB is different from the Asian Infrastructure Investment Bank (AIIB). To begin with there is difference in numbers. The AIIB comprises of over 50 prospective members. Secondly, unlike the BRICS, the member states of the AIIB are at very different levels of development; ranging from low-income (Bangladesh, Cambodia) to high-income (Australia, UK, Saudi Arabia). Such diversity prevents the possibility of creation of new political or economic structures founded on the AIIB. Secondly, the AIIB is poised to focus primarily on the development of major infrastructure projects. This gels well with China and the Asia Pacific Economic Cooperation (APEC)'s plans to improve regional connectivity in Asia. Thirdly, while the diverse membership of the AIIB allows for a blend of South-South and South-North co-operation, this could also result in logjam in case of difference of views (as has been the case with the World Trade Organization). For the BRICS, all members can be safely clubbed as large developing economies. The only exception is Russia, with its per capita GDP of US $ 24,800 qualifying as "high income" by World Bank standards. But the other BRICS economies are all "middle-income" by global criteria—in PPPs India's per capita GDP is US $ 5,900, China's US $ 12,900, South Africa's US $ 13,000, and Brazil's

US $ 16,000.[10] These figures can be interpreted to signify that the BRICS economies face similar developmental problems which in turn results in coherent and focused interests. A study by Ferdinand[11] analyzing the BRICS' countries' United Nations General Assembly (UNGA) voting data from 1974 to 2011, finds a considerable degree of cohesion among the BRICS that has not been changed by their institutionalization.

The NDB's forte is China's financial strength which is at a very close competition with the U.S. In 2014 China's total savings, measured at current exchange rates, were almost US $ 5.1 trillion compared to US $ 3.1 trillion for the U.S. China's almost US $ 2 trillion lead in savings compared to the U.S. means that China is already the world's superpower in financial terms.[12] The fact China is prepared to work with the other BRICS countries in the NDB provides huge startup leverage. Amongst the BRICS group, India, China and Russia are also home to trade corridors proposed in China's "Belt and Road" initiatives; thereby calling for further cooperation.

IMPACT ON SINO INDIAN RELATIONS

The influence and credibility of BRICS led multilateralism depend on its internal cohesion and harmony and this, in turn, revolves almost wholly on the state of relations between India and China.

While India and China share more than a dozen agreements across, trade, investment, energy, security, culture and education, the mutual suspicion of each other's geo political intentions, continue to cloud the relationship over the sixty five years of diplomatic relations. Both are aware that their economic growth has resulted in richer political dividends. Implicit in their foreign policy strategy to reach out both within and beyond the subcontinent, is the strong desire to act as a counterweight to the other's circle of influence. The warming of India's relations with the USA, Russia, Japan, member states of the ASEAN and so on, along with the steady modernization of Indian defense, is interpreted as an attempt to gain dominance over the Indo Pacific as a regional player. However a stable Sino Indian relation is critical for regional power balance and both the nations are aware of their responsibility to check any possibility of military confrontation in South Asia to ensure peaceful environment for economic and technological developments. Steps have already been taken to address the trust deficit, through visits by both heads of states and greater engagement in strategic dialogue and trade ties. The new leaders of India and China—Modi and Xi appear to be aggressive in forging out mutually beneficial partnerships towards greater strategic objectives.

China and India's engagement with each other on multilateral for a have facilitated better bilateral relations. An instance in support of the contention would be the Cancun 2010 Climate Change summit. The China-India bilateral cooperation and their cooperation under the BRICS framework are complementary to each other.[10] Some of the key projects include the BCIM Economic Corridor, the Chinese-style industrial parks in India, railway cooperation, and initiatives of the Silk Road Economic Belt and cooperation along the 21st Century Maritime Silk Road. Discussions are also on for a "Trans-Himalayas Economic Growth Region" driven by double-engine of China and India. India's accentuation of the 'Look East Act East' and China's move towards "good neighborhood policy"—both call for alliance building.

CONCLUSION

The development of large and effective BRICS institutions, like the BRICS bank and the Contingent Reserve Arrangement, can provide a valuable platform for the BRICS group in advancing reforms in the international financial and development architecture that favour developing and emerging countries in general. The AIIB, the NDB and the Silk Road Fund should therefore be viewed as complementary rather than substitutive to global and regional-development bank.

Key features of the new development finance institutions being created are worth highlighting. First, their creation implies an important shift in the international development finance architecture towards "Southern" or "Southern-dominated" institutions. This implies a reflection in the financial sphere of the changes that have been happening in manufacturing and other sectors. "Southern"—or developing and emerging—economies have assumed much larger roles; their status regarding macro-economic variables has also changed regarding, for example, their growing proportion of global savings and the foreign exchange reserves generated.

Secondly, some of these new institutions—particularly the AIIB and Silk Road Bank—imply a large role for China, a country that is also concentrating strongly on production in sectors such as world manufacturing and infrastructure capacity. It also holds a very high proportion of the savings and foreign exchange reserves of emerging and developing economies. (In this sense the NDB is different, in that the capital of the bank will be comprised of equal shares of the BRICS countries.)

Thirdly, it is interesting that the BRICS countries have actually chosen to create public development banks, in the same way that developed economies created such institutions in the post–Second World War period. Though clearly funded in the private capital markets—with co-financing from private and public lenders as well as private investors— the new development banks are owned and capitalized by national governments. These can therefore act as mechanism to implement and fund national, regional and global strategies of development.

Finally, the heterogeneity of the BRICS may prove not to be a weakness but strength. Through their joint and complementary efforts, wide-ranging, multi-level and high-quality economic cooperation, there will be greater convergence of the emerging markets, fueling the progress of the Asian century. With the New Development Bank, the BRICS make their first foray into collective global leadership and as long as China, India and other BRICS members insist on building their strong partnership, deepening economic cooperation, a better future is achievable for the BRICS.

REFERENCS

[1] Jim O Neill assigned the acronym BRIC to identify the four large countries, Brazil, Russia, India and China, that encompass over 40 percent of the world's population, and whose fast-growing economies best represent the beginning of a new era of emerging markets. S was added to include South Africa in 2010, another fast growing market.

[2] Jim O Neill assigned the acronym BRIC to identify the four large countries, Brazil, Russia, India and China, that encompass over 40 percent of the world's population, and whose fast-growing economies best represent the beginning of a new era of emerging markets. S was added to include South Africa in 2010, another fast growing market.

[3] Daniel Epstein, *New Development? The BRICS Bank and the International System*, January 2, 2015, Harvard International Review; http://hir.harvard.edu/new-development-the-brics-bank-and-the-international-system

[4] Vijayakumar, Sanjay, *The building of the BRICS bank*, May 18, 2015, http://www.thehindu.com/business/the-building-of-the-brics-bank/article7214558.ece

Bhattacharya, A., M. Romani and N. Stern (2012). "Infrastructure for development: meeting the challenge", Policy Paper, June. Centre for Climate Change Economics and Policy,

Grantham Research Institute on Climate Change and the Environment in collaboration with G-24.

[5] A Brics Development Bank: A Dream Coming True?, UNCTAD Discussion Paper No. 215, March 2014 http://unctad.org/en/PublicationsLibrary/osgdp20141_en.pdf

[6] A Brics Development Bank: A Dream Coming True?, UNCTAD Discussion Paper No. 215, March 2014 http://unctad.org/en/PublicationsLibrary/osgdp20141_en.pdf Bhattacharya, A., Romani, M. and Stern, N. (2012). "Infrastructure for development: meeting the challenge", Policy Paper, June. Centre for Climate Change Economics and Policy, Grantham Research Institute on Climate Change and the Environment in collaboration with G-24.

[7] Liu, Qiao; Lejot, Paul and Arner, Douglas W., *Finance in Asia: Institutions, Regulation and Policy*, Routledge Publication, 2013; pp. 518–519.

[8] https://www.cia.gov/library/publications/the-world-factbook/fields/ 2004.html

[9] Ross, John, "BRICS Bank Can be World-Changing," June 15, 2015, www.china.org.cn

[10] Younis, M., Watson, N. and Spratt, S. (2013). What next for the BRICS bank? Rapid Response Briefing. Institute of Development Studies. Available at: http://opendocs.ids.ac.uk/opendocs/ bitstream/handle/123456789/3270/ Rapid%203.pdf.

[11] Wei Wei, "BRICS is Also Significant for Indo-China Ties", The Economic Times, Jul 15, 2014.

[12] Ferdinand, P. (2014a). Rising powers at the UN: an analysis of the voting behaviour of BRICS in the General Assembly. Third World Quarterly, 35(3), 376–391.

Ferdinand, P. (2014b). Foreign Policy Convergence in Pacific Asia: The Evidence from Voting in the UN General Assembly. The British Journal of Politics & International Relations, 16(4), 662–679.

BIBLIOGRAPHY/REFERENCES

1. Armijo, L.E. (2007). The BRICS Countries (Brazil, Russia, India, and China) as an Analytical Category: Mirage or Insight? Asian Perspective, 31(4), 7–42.

2. Armijo, L.E. and Roberts, C. (2014). The Emerging Powers and Global Governance: Why the BRICS Matter. In R. E. Looney (Ed.), Routledge International Handbooks. Handbook of emerging economies (pp. 503–524).
3. Brütsch, C. and Papa, M. (2013). Deconstructing the BRICS: Bargaining Coalition, Imagined Community, or Geopolitical Fad? The Chinese Journal of International Politics, 6(3), 299–327.
4. Chan, S. (2008). China, the US and power-transition theory: A critique. London, New York, NY: Routledge.
5. Flemes, D. (2011). India-Brazil-South Africa (IBSA) in the New Global Order: Interests, Strategies and Values of the Emerging Coalition. International Studies, 46(4), 401–421.
6. Hurrell, A. (2006). Hegemony, liberalism and global order: what space for would-be great powers? International Affairs, 82(1), 1–19.
7. Laïdi, Z. (2012). BRICS: Sovereignty power and weakness. International Politics, 49(5), 614–632.
8. Looney, R.E. (Ed.) (2014). Routledge International Handbooks. Handbook of emerging economies, New York, NY.
9. Pant, H.V. (2013). The BRICS Fallacy. The Washington Quarterly, 36(3), 91–105.
10. Roberts, C. (2009). Russia's BRICs Diplomacy: Rising Outsider with Dreams of an Insider. Polity, 42(1), 38–73.
11. Stuenkel, O. (2013). The Financial Crisis, Contested Legitimacy, and the Genesis of Intra-BRICS Cooperation. Global Governance, 19, 611–630.

Acronyms

ADB	Asian Development Bank
ADIZ	Air Defence Identification Zone
AIIB	Asia Infrastructure Investment Bank
APEC	Asia Pacific Economic Cooperation
APIs	Active Pharmaceutical Ingredients
ASEAN	Association of Southeast Asian Nations
BCIM	Bangladesh China India Myanmar
BIG B	Bay of Bengal Industrial Growth Belt
CNPC	Chinese National Petroleum Corporation
CRA	Contingency Reserve Arrangements
EAEU	Eurasian Economic Union
ECI	Economic Complexity Index
FLAR	Fondo Latino Americano de Reserve
FTAAP	Free Trade Agreement in Asia Pacific
GVCs	Global Value Chains
HRA	High Risk Area
ICJ	International Court of Justice
IOR	Indian Ocean Region
ISPS	International Ship and Port Security Code
LAC	Line of Actual Control
MDA	Maritime Domain Awareness
MFN	Most Favored Nation
MOFCOM	Ministry of Commerce
MSR	Maritime Silk Road

NDB	New Development Bank
OBOR	One Belt One Road
PCMSP	Privately Contracted Maritime Security Professionals
PFM	Perspective Funding Member
PNG	Papua New Guinea
POK	Pakistan Occupied Kashmir
PRC	People's Republic of China
RCEP	Regional Comprehensive Economic Partnership
RCI	Regional Cooperation and Integration
RECP	Regional Economic Cooperation Partnership
RTAs	Regional Trading Agreements
SAARC	South Asian Association for Regional Cooperation
SCS	South China Sea
SEA	Southeast Asian
SLOC	Sea Lines of Communications
SREB	Silk Route Economic Belt
THECs	Trans-Himalayan Economic Corridors
TTIP	Transatlantic Trade and Investment Partnership
TPP	Trans-Pacific Partnership
TTIP	Transatlantic Trade and Investment partnership
UNGA	United Nations General Assembly
WEF	World Economic Forum
XUAR	Xinjiang Uighur Autonomous Region